Endorsements

My immediate response after reading this book was: "I don't believe most people have ever read such a succinct, yet comprehensive, biblical presentation of what makes the Good News truly good." I could almost title Tuck's book: Hearing the Gospel for the First Time. Key words like reconciliation are unwrapped with skill, scholarship, and pastoral compassion. You will find in these pages a full Gospel for real people living in a real world.

I can promise that you will come to a new understanding of many biblical characters who are now simply names. The sweep of Christ's love in the context of God's eternal role of redemption will give new perspective on the entire Bible and especially in the life and ministry of Paul. I recommend Sharing the Good News as a must read in a world that has mostly lost the true message and meaning of the church. This may be the best book in defense of the Gospel that I have ever read.

Dr. Ronald Higdon, pastor emeritus of Broadway Baptist Church, Louisville, KY. Author of Faith Never Stands Alone and other books.

With the declining numbers in church attendance, a reality compounded by the COVID-19 pandemic, William Powell Tuck, who believes in the importance of being together as a community of faith, pushing back against current trends, draws on the entire biblical story to invite the church to reclaim its calling to proclaim the good news that in Jesus Christ God is reconciling the world to God's self. In these chapters, each of which explores a biblical story, we discover the importance of carrying out the church's missional calling.

Robert D. Cornwall, Minister-at-Large, Christian Church (Disciples of Christ), author of many books including Unfettered Spirit: Spiritual Gifts for the New Great Awakening

The author of this book is right, Covid did disrupt most of our churches and congregations in their missions, and now we are wondering about how to regain the ground we have lost and repair the broken connections many of us have experienced.

In his best and always welcome pastoral mode, William Tuck has wisely assayed the situation and offers invaluable suggestions in this timely book about how we can get back on track again with our important mission as the church. Hopefully, as he indicates, we can come back even better and stronger than we were before the pandemic, for the testing of the church almost always causes us to rethink many things and then reconstitute ourselves in the most helpful ways.

As always, the author's down-home, simply expressed stories and illustrations from a lifetime of pastoring are in themselves worth the price of the book, and often linger pleasantly and compellingly in the mind long after we have read them.

I recently had lunch with the very thoughtful and creative pastor of the little Methodist church to which I now belong, and we were discussing what we might do to improve our own church's stressed and harried situation in a post-Covid world. Now that I have read this book, I can hardly wait for it to appear in print so I can obtain a copy for him. He will love it, as I'm sure all pastors will.

John Killinger, former pastor and professor at Vanderbilt, Chicago, Princeton, and Samford University, and author of many books including *Fundamentals of Preaching*

Whether it is helping one learn how to face grief and death or explaining the intricacies of a particular faith tradition or confronting heresies regarding the end-times that need to be left behind once and for all, my seminary preaching professor and mentor, Bill Tuck, always provides insightful wisdom to motivate the church in her local expression as she faces a multiplicity of challenging issues, especially in these constantly changing days of the third decade of the twenty-first century. This volume on evangelism is no exception to his insightful wisdom. The book is well-researched and well-written. It is obvious Tuck has prayerfully reflected upon what he has researched and written in *Sharing the Good News: The Church's Charge for Missions*. One quickly gleans his insightful wisdom is theologically, biblically, and ethically sound – insightful wisdom that will move the body of Christ from complacency to urgency, especially in a time that has been (and still is) plagued with COVID-19 and one that is charged with political idolatry. Enlivened by the Holy One, Dr. Tuck reminds readers of the need to re-engage the Great Commission and heed God's call to follow biblical paradigms with creativity for proclaiming the Good News of the Kingdom of God in all those places where it is news. This book, like all his others, helps, explains how, and challenges us to be about the task of sharing the Good News. Taking Bill Tuck's insightful wisdom seriously will re-energize the church for faithful testimony in the future.

Jimmy Gentry, *Senior Pastor*
Garden Lakes Baptist Church
Rome, Georgia

Other Books by William Powell Tuck

Facing Grief and Death

The Struggle for Meaning (editor)

Knowing God: Religious Knowledge in the Theology of John Baillie

Our Baptist Tradition

Ministry: An Ecumenical Challenge (editor)

Getting Past the Pain

A Glorious Vision

The Bible as Our Guide for Spiritual Growth (editor)

Authentic Evangelism

The Lord's Prayer Today

The Way for All Seasons

Through the Eyes of a Child

Christmas Is for the Young…Whatever Their Age

Love as a Way of Living

The Compelling Faces of Jesus

The Left Behind Fantasy

The Ten Commandments: Their Meaning Today

Facing Life's Ups and Downs

The Church in Today's World

The Church Under the Cross

Modern Shapers of Baptist Thought in America

The Journey to the Undiscovered Country: What's Beyond Death?

A Pastor Preaching: Toward a Theology of the Proclaimed Word

The Pulpit Ministry of the Pastors of River Road Church, Baptist
(editor)

The Last Words from the Cross

Lord, I Keep Getting a Busy Signal:
Reaching for a Better Spiritual Connection

Overcoming Sermon Block: The Preacher's Workshop

A Revolutionary Gospel:
Salvation in the Theology of Walter Rauschenbusch

Holidays, Holy Days, and Special Days

A Positive Word for Christian Lamenting: Funeral Homilies

The Forgotten Beatitude: Worshipping through Stewardship

Star Thrower: A Pastor's Handbook

A Pastoral Prophet: Sermons and Prayers of Wayne E. Oates (editor)

The Abiding Presence: Communion Meditations

Which Voice Will You Follow?

Beginning and Ending a Pastorate

The Difficult Sayings of Jesus

Conversations with My Grandchildren about God, Religion, and Life

Markers Along the Way: The Signs of Jesus in the Gospel of John

The Rebirth of the Church

Jesus' Journey to the Cross

Lessons from Old Testament Characters

Stories that Continue to Speak to Us Today:
Looking Again at the Parables of Jesus

Challenges for Today's Living: Studies in 1 Corinthians

About the Author

William Powell Tuck, a native of Virginia, has served as a pastor, seminary professor, college professor, interim pastor, and intentional interim pastor. He is the author of more than forty books including Challenges for Today's Living and The Rebirth of the Church. He has received a Doctor of Divinity degree from the University of Richmond, in 1999 he received the Medallion Award from the national Boys and Girls Club of America, in 1997 The Pastor of the Year Award from the Academy of Parish Clergy, and in 2016 received the Wayne Oates Award from the Oates Institute in Louisville, Kentucky. He and his wife, Emily, are the parents of two children and five grandchildren, and live in Richmond, Virginia.

Sharing the Good News

The Church's Charge for Missions

William Powell Tuck

Energion Publications
Cantonment, Florida
2024

Copyright © 2024, William Powell Tuck. All rights reserved.

Portions of some chapters are revisions from articles originally in The Religious Herald. Portions of some other chapters are revisions from articles originally in The Advanced Bible Study (1980), used by permission of Lifeway Publications. Special appreciation to the Virginia Baptist Historical Society for assistance in transcribing the articles from The Religious Herald and The Advanced Bible Study and the assistance of Greg Gunther.

Unless otherwise noted, Scripture quotations are from Revised Standard Version of the Bible, copyright © 1946, 1952, and 1971 National Council of the Churches of Christ in the United States of America. Used by permission. All rights reserved worldwide.

Scripture quotations marked Moffatt are from "The Holy Bible Containing the Old and New Testaments, a New Translation" by James Moffatt.

Scripture quotations marked TEV are from the Good News Translation in Today's English Version-Second Edition. Copyright © 1992 by American Bible Society. Used by Permission.

Scripture Quotations marked Phil or Phillips are from The New Testament in Modern English, Copyright © 1958 by J. B. Phillips.

Scripture quotations marked NEB are taken from the New English Bible, copyright © Cambridge University Press and Oxford University Press 1961,1970. All rights reserved.

Some Scripture quotations are from the Authorized King James Version, Oxford University Press.

Some Scripture quotations are the author's own translation.

Chapter Header Image: Photo 80943358 | Cross © Arybickii | Dreamstime.com

ISBN: 978-1-63199-897-3
eISBN: 978-1-63199-898-0
Library of Congress Control Number: 2024935786

Energion Publications
1241 Conference Rd
Cantonment, FL 32533
energion.com
pubs@energion.com

In
Memory of
Kenneth Glass
And
In appreciation of
Connie Glass
Who both responded to the
Call of missions

Table of Contents

Preface vii

1. Christ's Commission to the Church 1
2. Two Early Home & Foreign Missionaries 7
3. Preparing for the Messiah 13
4. Grace for Sinners 23
5. Putting Persons Before Traditions 33
6. The Radical Demand of Agape 43
7. The Sweep of Christ's Love 53
8. God's Eternal Role of Redemption 61
9. Sharing Christ's Name to the World 65
10. Paul's Method of Witnessing 71
11. Undergirding Missions with Prayer & Giving 77
12. Witnessing: The Way of Missions Under the Guidance of the Holy Spirit ... 83
13. Reasons for Attending Church 89
14. What's Our Business Outside The Building? 99

PREFACE

Many churches are concerned about the absent parishioners who have not returned to worship after the end of the COVID pandemic. Why have they not come back? Many reasons could fill our imagination. Some enjoyed watching worship services on zoom while in their pajamas. Others may use the time to shop, visit friends or relatives, enjoy recreation pursuits, rest, or dozens of other things. Now it is hard to forsake those habits and return to church. They should be contacted by one's church, but scolding or arguing with them will not be helpful. For some to restart their habit of worship may be difficult. Some may have joined those who say they are "spiritual" but no longer need corporate worship. Some no longer feel the church offers them any genuine benefits anymore. They may have linked their lives with the many others who have chosen the path of secularism. But some still feel a sense of connectedness. "I tend to fall back on a sense of being spiritual. I believe we're all connected to the universe in some way," William Shatner states. "and we're learning more about those connections every day, but we don't have all the answers by any means. I believe in the mystery: the awesome question of why we're here and how we're connected."[1]

I personally do not believe that it is possible to grow spiritually as a Christian apart from the church. Peter Marty reminds us of Dietrich Bonhoeffer's idea that "there is no way to know Christ apart from Christian community. *Christus als Gemeinde existierend*--Christ exists as community." The church is the place we meet the living Christ.[2] Our challenge is to remind persons of the One

---

[1] William Shatner, with Joshua Brando. *Boldly Go: Reflections on a Life of Awe and Wonder* (New York: Atria Books, 2022), 34.
[2] Peter W. Marty, "Why Aren't People Coming Back?" *The Christian Century* (December 2022), 1.

in whom we find redemption and eternal life and the uniqueness of the church as the community where we meet and grow in him. This summons us to the initial commission of Jesus to share the Good News of the Gospel with others and encourage them to be a part of the community of faith. As new believers commit their lives to Christ, hopefully, this awakening will encourage latent church members to rejoin the community of faith. The epidemic of loneliness in the United States is rampant, and many long for what the church can offer in its community. Our summons to challenge the absent church members to a renewal of their faith does not lessen our commission to reach into our neighborhood and the world beyond with the Gospel but deepens that command.

The following chapters note the preparation for the coming of the Messiah, bear witness to our Savior, Jesus Christ, the depth and scope of Christ's *agape* love and grace, God's eternal goal in redemption, early mission endeavors, Paul's method of witnessing, the guidance of the Holy Spirit, the importance of the church's continued response to its call to share the good news about Christ, and the ongoing challenge of our mission obligation. If the church fails its mission responsibility, who will possibly bear that message? These chapters boldly assert the challenge for the church to continue aggressively in its commission to proclaim the Gospel message. The church moves forward in the assurance that Christ continues to work through the lives of his followers to proclaim boldly the Good News of the hope of life eternal through Christ our Lord. I extend my appreciation to my fellow minister and friend, Rand Forder, for proofreading my original manuscript.

CHRIST'S COMMISSION TO THE CHURCH
2 Corinthians 5:14-6:2

Even in an age when men or women are able to orbit the moon, and their scientific and intellectual achievements are dazzling, humanity still seems to have lost its sense of spiritual direction. Individuals have not learned how to live with themselves or each other or God.

SEARCHING FOR DIRECTIONS

Daily we are confronted with questions dealing with the meaning of life. The questions will not and cannot remain hidden. War, suffering, poverty, suicide, drug addiction, alcoholism, pain, and death have all marched across the line of our contemporary vision, and we are unable to ignore them. They are here; and they are real. They haunt us; bother us; chill us; frighten us; confuse us; and challenge us. We are not sure who we are or where we are going. Carl Sandburg is correct. Man/woman has a "menagerie" inside his/her ribs. Man/woman is a paradox and a bundle of contradictions; he/she is a Dr. Jekyll and Mr. Hyde character. Our basic sin of self-centeredness has estranged us from God, oneself, and others. The apostle Paul has stated the dilemma. "I do not understand my own actions. For I do not do what I want, but I do the very thing I hate" (Rom. 7:15).

Many of those who are searching for life's meaning are experiencing frustration, loneliness, loss of purpose and have turned away from the church. Stephen Bullivant, a British sociologist, in his recent book, *Nonverts: The Making of Ex-Christian America,* notes that nearly a third of Americans now claim no religious affiliation. Some have turned away from the church because of its reaction to the rise of the political ultra-conservative religious right's view of Christian nationalism. In his book, Bullivant states three basic developments that influenced this happening. First, for decades the Cold War and the threat of godless communism caused people to be reluctant to disclose that they were nonreligious. By the mid-2000's, however, people began to feel that it was no longer unpatriotic to declare that one was nonreligious. A second factor he notes is the "sudden appearance of the internet" which made it possible for persons who felt nonreligious to find others who agreed with their perspective no matter where one might live. People could now converse with others who felt as they did. The third reason he suggests is what he calls "the herd factor." Since others are becoming nonreligious, that seems to draw other likeminded thinkers to join the crowd. [3]

An interesting fact, however, is that Bullivant himself, who grew up in a nonreligious home and was originally a nonbeliever, came under the influence of some Dominicans who invited him regularly for dinner. Since the Dominicans had to go to Mass before dinner, he started attending Mass as well. He saw that the Dominicans lived what they believed, and he eventually asked to be baptized and became a Catholic. So, the nonbeliever became a believer because of the influence of the Dominican believers on him. Bullivant himself becomes an example of what can happen to a nonbeliever when one is exposed to the Gospel even over a meal.[4] When he was exposed to the Gospel in a community of faith, he was drawn to their fellowship of faith. The Good News can be shared in many means and ways.

---

3 Stephen Bullivant, *Nonverts: The Making of Ex-Christian America,* (New York: Oxford University Press, 2022).
4 *Ibid.*

Reconciled to God

At the heart of the Christian faith is the good news of reconciliation. Today more than ever, the message of salvation needs to be shared with the nonreligious person next door or around the world, in ways of old or in completely new methods. The biblical concept of salvation refers not only to victory over sin but to the wholeness, healing, and fullness one can receive in Christ (John 11:25-26; Rom. 14:17-19; Eph. 2:11-14). In Christ our brokenness. neurosis, meaninglessness, turmoil, and despair are overcome. In the "holiness" of God's love through Christ, those who are searching for purpose and meaning in life can find redemption and "wholeness." Communion with God opens up for us a restoration which enables us to understand our self and live in fellowship with others. Everyone longs for this wholeness. Non-religiousness carries an emptiness within which needs filling. I believe only the Gospel can truly fill that void.

The Greek word for reconciliation occurs only in five Pauline passages in the New Testament. (Rom. 5: 10-11; 11:15; 2 Cor. 5:18-20; Col. 1:20-22, Eph. 2:16). But the idea is expressed throughout the New Testament and is used to denote the restoration of the relationship between humanity and God. The root meaning is concerned with a "change" or that which is made "different." Our sin separates us from God. Even at our very best, we must realize that a great chasm separates us from God. In divine holiness God is "wholly other." Since God's nature is so radically different from ours, the initiative in reconciliation and redemption comes from God, not us. God has bridged the chasm caused by humanity's sin. In one of his classes Dr. Frank Stagg, the New Testament scholar, gave a vivid description of what the term mediator indicates when applied to Christ. He said that Jesus was not someone who stood between God and man/woman, but God came to "overcome the betweenness" between God and man/woman. In Christ God restores a relationship which we had broken by our rebellion and sin.

God's Eternal Love Draws Humanity

It should be noted that Paul is clear in his understanding that it is man and woman who are being reconciled to God. It was man/woman not God who had broken the fellowship. Humanity is the object of reconciliation, while God is the active subject, who has continued to love man/woman in spite of his or her sin. We do not need to appease or pacify an angry God. The cross revealed the heart of God's eternal love for all persons. Who and what is God like? Jesus answered that question with his life and death. God the Father is like the Son who cares so much for his lost children that he actively seeks them out wherever they are. The parables of the lost sheep, the lost coin, and the prodigal son are word pictures that express the deep compassion and eternal vigil of God. The message of the incarnation is not that God remained coolly detached from the world, but that God was personally involved in the world through Christ. "God was in Christ reconciling the world to himself" (2 Cor. 5:19).

The Church as the Agent of Reconciliation

The central task of the Church, as the witnessing community, is to be the agent of reconciliation. The Church's ministry is a ministry of reconciliation: to proclaim the redemptive love of God. The responsibility of those who have been reconciled is to be ambassadors on behalf of Christ. We were created to have fellowship with God and outside this relationship there is only death. Just as an ambassador speaks for and represents one's country, so the Christian is God's spokesperson in the world with the message of the newness of life that is available in Jesus Christ. The responsibility for carrying the message of God's reconciliation rest upon the shoulders of "the people of God." The Greek word for people is "*laos*," from which our English words "laymen" and "laity" are derived. In the original sense a layman is one who has been called out by God for his or her special task in the world. All Christians are "called out" to share in the ministry of reconciliation. God has taken the initiative to overcome our estrangement and now the reconciled are commissioned to a vocation of sharing the good news.

Two Early Home & Foreign Missionaries
Amos 7:14-15; 5:4-6; 11-14; 9:9-11

Sometimes we can be greatly aroused or angered by certain social or political injustices that we see or read about in the newspapers or see on social media. We often wonder why someone does not do something to correct such sad conditions. Seldom, however, are we aroused enough to initiate action ourselves. We will talk about it, "gripe" about it, maybe even curse about it, but rarely will we be motivated enough to become personally involved. Amos is an example of a man who was not content to talk about problems but was spurred into action by a deep sense of concern. Although a citizen of the southern kingdom of Judah, Amos turns to his northern neighbors in Israel and proclaims God's judgment against their licentious and corrupt practices. He saw a mission field in the backyard of his divided nation.

Amos, the Lay Prophet

Amos did not suffer from the popular heresy, which is prevalent today, that only "professional" holy men or preachers have the responsibility of speaking about religious matters. Amos denied that he was a member of the professional prophet's guilds or the son of a prophet. He was a layman who earned his living by raising sheep and desert figs. Amos claimed that he was not like the professional prophet, Amaziah, who told King Jeroboam II only what he wanted to hear, but that he was God's own spokesman to Israel. His message was one of divine judgment, and he was compelled to speak.

The Church Under Criticism

Over the past few years much criticism has been directed against the church. Some book titles suggest the problem— "The Comfortable Pew," "The Empty Pulpit," "The Noise of Solemn Assemblies," and "The Captivity of the Church." Most of these studies have been extremely challenging to today's church. It is interesting to observe that many of these books discuss the major role which the lay ministry must play in the Church if its mission of converting the world is to be accomplished. The ordained clergy and the layman are both a part of what the New Testament calls "a peculiar people" (I Peter 2:9). They both are a part of the working crew of the Church. There is no such thing as a spectator Christian. All Christians are ministers in their own right to be the salt, light, and leaven in the world to preserve it from spiritual and moral decay.

The Priesthood of Believers

The concept of the priesthood of the believers involves the knowledge that we have one ministry but many forms, shapes, talents, and gifts. Amos was willing to undertake his ministry in the eighth century. Now the church needs to recover its mission in the twentieth-first century; that is the role of the lay ministry again.

God's Judgment

The nation Israel had misunderstood its covenant relationship to God and believed that its prosperity was a sign of God's approval. Fearlessly Amos spoke out against the economic, social, cultural, political, and religious injustices which were offensive before God. The dominant theme of the message was one of God's judgments upon their sins. God's judgment would sift Israel in its captivity like the chaff is removed from corn.

The righteous would be preserved while the sinful element would be destroyed (Amos 1:3). Amos holds out words of hope to those who will seek God. Hope is possible for those who will search for God without looking for selfish gains from him. Amos's message was clear. Men and women could not hide behind masks from God. God required righteousness above religiosity. Ritual and traditions cannot cover a person's social sins. Without justice and righteousness in one's everyday life, his or her religion is only a cover for hypocrisy.

Religion Should Embrace All of One's Life

The lesson from the message of the eighth-century prophet should be clear but it has usually been tragically ignored. Our religion, however, cannot be hung up with our Sunday clothes. The religious life cannot be compartmentalized. It must be an invasion of our whole lives. We cannot be concerned only with a private faith and personal morality, but our faith must have wider bounds to include our community, nation, and world. Our worship inside our church buildings becomes idolatrous unless it touches our everyday living. The scriptures remind us again today that God expects the Christian not to turn one's back on the problems of the inner cities, poverty, war, race, unemployment relations, and other social needs. The Christian's faith demands that our religion touch the whole world. We may sometimes get dirty, but those who are the salt of the earth will minister to the world only as they are involved in it. Wherever the church scatters in the world, its worship becomes service, and its service becomes worship if its faith is vital and real.

An Unwilling Foreign Missionary: Jonah

Jonah 1:1-3, 3:1-5, 10 to 4:3, 9-11

Although Jonah is one of the best known of all the Old Testament books, it is probably one of the least understood. It is a shame that most readers miss its great message and get caught on the fish story. The book of Jonah has some of the highest theological insights found in the Old Testament and contains a message that is closer to the New Testament emphasis than any in the Old Testament. The figure of Jonah is one of the most frequent that appears on the walls of the Catacombs depicting early Christian art.

A Parable of Israel

In New Testament times, Jonah was so highly regarded that Jesus said concerning himself that One greater than Jonah had come (Matt. 14:9). To some, the story of Jonah is an ingenious tale of a man's attempt to avoid God's will. Others see it only as an interesting ancient narrative with an almost comical note. Still others have perceived that the book differs from the oracles delivered by other Old Testament prophets and focuses instead on the story of the personal struggle of a prophet. The story of Jonah, however, is more than merely the account of a prophet's neglect of his personal responsibility to God. I believe that Jonah's struggle is a parable of Israel's failure as the Covenant people of Jehovah.

The Call to Awaken a Nation

In order to understand the message of Jonah, one needs to recall that Israel had experienced a succession of foreign conquerors — Assyria, Babylonia, and Persia. During this time Israel had endured the Exile and now felt only a spirit of bitterness and vindictiveness toward other nations. Israel had suffered so much from the hands of numerous enemies that their only desire was to see God's judgment and wrath brought down upon them and utterly destroy them. Israel had lost sight of its missionary task as God's Covenant people and had developed a narrow provincialism and rigid Jewish nationalism. God was depicted as their private redeemer, who was unconcerned about the rest of humankind. Their religion had become self-centered, legalistic, ritualistic, and callous. The prophet's task was to find a way to awaken the nation to their missionary commission. His weapon was a missionary tract or parable.

Jonah Tries to Avoid His Mission

An unknown author, writing probably in the fourth century, centers his story around an obscure figure named Jonah, the son of Amittai, who lived in Israel in the period of Jeroboam II (786-746 B.C.) (2 Kings 14:25). When Jonah is commanded by God to preach against the wickedness of Nineveh, an Assyrian city, he takes a ship going in the opposite direction toward a Spanish port named Tarshish. Jonah, however, finds that he is unable to run away from God. After a series of calamities at sea, and his "swallowing" experience with a whale, Jonah receives a second chance to proclaim God's judgment against Nineveh. This time he obeys the command and much to his surprise the whole city repents. In his compassion, God forgives the Ninevites. Instead of rejoicing at the repentance of the Ninevites and their divine deliverance, Jonah is angry and bitter. He wanted to witness their destruction, not their salvation. While waiting outside the city to see God's action, Jonah rests in the shade provided by a large gourd plant. The plant withers and dies the next day, and Jonah expresses anger at its destruction. The absolute absurdity of Jonah's position is revealed in his pity for the gourd plant, which had grown up in a day and then died, and at the same time, his lack of compassion for the hundreds of people God spared in the Assyrian city.

The Folly of Rejecting God's Commission

The lesson of the parable becomes clear at the end of the story. In disapproving of Jonah's behavior, the hearer soon finds that one has judged himself or herself. The parable of the good Samaritan in the New Testament was used in this same way by Jesus. Jonah becomes a mirror in which Israel sees the rejection of the missionary commission of God. Israel is warned that its rigid exclusiveness denotes its renouncement of the God of Abraham, Isaac, and Jacob.

THE DIMENSION OF GOD'S LOVE

In the small book of Jonah, the writer has established some eternal truths about God. God is depicted as one who has dominion over the whole world, the land, and the sea, the Gentile as well as the Jew. God's love is also a universal love that grants forgiveness to all people of all races and cultures who will repent and turn to God. In repudiating its missionary concern for other nations, Israel revealed its misunderstanding of its covenant with God. Israel was chosen for the purpose of serving as God's instrument to proclaim his redemption to all the world. Israel turned its back on the God of the Covenant when it attempted to make God's grace its private possession. God's love is not for special privilege but is lost if it is not shared.

In the great commission of Jesus, he has warned his followers against exclusiveness when he proclaimed: "go ... and make disciples of all nations" (Matt. 28:19).

Preparing for the Messiah
Luke 3:1-3

Driving along a highway last winter I passed a sign which read: "Caution: Men at Work." As I rounded a curve, I soon saw state workers engaged in removing a huge pile of fallen rocks from the road. The sign had cautioned me of their presence, and I had slowed down to prepare for what might be awaiting me on the road ahead. I often wonder if it would not help all of us as we travel along the road of life to be aware of another sign: "Caution: God at Work." God is indeed, you know. God is at work everywhere. Unfortunately, we do not always have eyes that are open to the divine Presence.

Luke erected a caution sign to warn his readers about the God who was at work bringing in his kingdom. From his desert pulpit, John the Baptist summoned men and women to repentance for the coming of a New Age. Here was a prophet pointing his people to the sign of God's presence among them.

All of the Gospel writers, including Luke, were aware that some of the Baptist's disciples thought that he was the long-awaited Messiah. Luke pointedly contrasted the roles of Jesus and John. He noted the great significance of John's prophetic ministry but carefully underscored that its purpose was to prepare the way for Jesus who was the Messiah. John rightfully had "to decrease and Jesus had to increase."

A Historical Orientation

For four centuries the voice of prophecy had been silent in Israel. Many of the Israelites had begun to wonder if God had not forsaken them. Then the prophet, John the Baptist, began to speak. The sudden and dramatic appearance of the Baptist was to the people a clear sign that the messianic age was about to dawn. The Hebrew people believed that prophecy would arise again before the Messiah came (Mal. 4:5). Luke described John's call to his prophetic ministry in the same words used of Old Testament prophets: "the word of God came to John" (3:2). For some passages in the Old Testament that describe the prophets' call in a similar way, see Samuel 15:10, I Kings 17:2, or Jeremiah 2:1. John's venture was not self-initiated but came as a response to the moving of God within his life.

As a historian, Luke considered John's appearance so significant that he fixed its exact date with six designations. He carefully noted the political and religious leaders who were in power when John arose. Nailing his story down within the secular context of his day, Luke began with the Roman emperor, Tiberius and then named the local governors and other civil and ecclesiastical leaders.

In a sense it might have seemed confusing to have named two high priests since only one could be serving at a time. A high priest technically was supposed to serve for life but often they were deposed by the Romans. Although Annas had been deposed in A.D. 15 and his son-in-law, Caiaphas was now high priest, many believed that the deposed Annas was still the real power behind the scene. In referring to rulers in Rome and the surrounding areas of Palestine, Luke intimated the universal significance of what he was writing. "To Luke," William Barclay observes, "the emergence of John the Baptist was one of the hinges on which history turned."[5] It is ironic that as history has moved on, the names of

---

5 William Barclay, *The Gospel of Luke* (Philadelphia; The Westminster Press, 1956). 26.

A CLARION CALL TO REPENTANCE (3:3-6)

When John preached, he expected a response. His voice rang with shattering directness. His message was forceful and clear. The great moment of God's coming kingdom was drawing near. If individuals were to prepare for his coming, decisive action from them would be necessary. Moral obstacles had to be overcome. Men and women must repent of their sins if they were to be ready to receive the "Coming One." John's ministry is depicted as a fulfillment of the prediction of the prophet Isaiah who described the one to prepare "the way of the Messiah as the voice of one crying in the wilderness" (Is.40:3-5). When a monarch in those ancient times traveled into remote sections of his kingdom, heralds were sent ahead to announce his coming. Highways had to be prepared for him to travel over. This meant that valleys had to be filled in and hills lowered. Crooked places had to be straightened and rough places made smooth (vv. 4-5).

John was the herald telling the people that the king was coming. His word to them was "prepare your lives as you would prepare the roads to receive a king." To do this you must repent of your sins. Repentance here means more than merely a "change of mind." Repentance involves a turning from sin to God; it entails sorrow for your sins and confession of them. Repentance means righting wrongs and establishing righteousness in our relationships to others. If the people will respond. "all flesh shall see the salvation of God." (v.6).

John's call for a "baptism of repentance" was directed to his own people. According to an old rabbinical saying, "If Israel would repent only one day, the Son of David would come forthwith." The phrase "even now the axe is laid to the root of the trees" (v. 9) expressed the concept that the tree was valued for its fruit. If it did not produce fruit, it would be cut down. Judgment is inevitable for those who do not live lives that give evidence of repentance.

Many of the Jews thought that when the Messiah came, he would bring his judgment upon the Gentiles, but they would escape this judgment because they were descendants of Abraham. John made clear that his call for repentance was issued to all. No nation, not even Israel, could escape God's judgment. They, too, had to reaffirm their relationship to God by repentance and baptism. Jews, in essence, were put in the same category as Gentiles (vv. 8-9).

Baptism had been an act that the Jews reserved for Gentiles who were converted to Judaism. Proselytes, Gentile converts, were immersed in water, and then the men had to be circumcised. Others, like the Essenes, may have practiced immersion at this time also. Tolbert believes that the baptism practiced by John and the early Christians was distinctive.[6] There seems to be little question that John's baptism must have been different from the practices of others or why would he have received the designation as "the baptizer?" As many of the ancient prophets had done, John used a dramatic sign to show that a sinner had begun a new way of life.

John's words had been severe (v. 7) because he knew that people usually wanted to escape impending judgment but were often unwilling to turn from their sins. He probably immersed the professed penitent in the Jordan River. Those he baptized may have formed themselves into a sort of community which was preparing for the coming kingdom. Some scholars have suggested that John's call for baptism was not just a focus upon an individual act. It was a dramatic expression of a commitment to the impending messianic kingdom. It was a challenge to identify themselves with a new order of things.[7] Baptism, in and of itself, did not impart salvation. It was not a magical rite that could make the person safe when judgment came. Repentance required a changed life that gave evidence in a person's daily living that he or she had really

---

6   Malcolm O. Tolbert, "Luke " *The Broadman Bible Commentary* (Nashville: Broadman Press, 1958) Vol. 9, 36.
7   Walter Rauschenbusch, *A Theology for the Social Gospel*, (New York: The Macmillan Co., 1918), 197-8.

repented. No mere form or ceremony was sufficient. Evidence of this changed life would be seen in very practical ways (vv. 20-25). Repent of your sins was not just a generalization. John got specific and named some sins, so they would all understand the concreteness and realness of his demand. Only when individuals recognize their sins from which they must turn can they "bear fruits that befit repentance" (v. 8).

Sometimes it seems obvious that many within the church have not moved far beyond the misunderstanding which some had of John's baptism and his call for repentance. Christian baptism for some is little more than a magic rite. A woman actually said to me once, "I don't have to attend church or be concerned about the way I live because I have been baptized." For her, baptism was simply a magical act. It gave her salvation, she mistakenly thought, without requiring commitment, worship, or service. But think how far this attitude is from the teachings of the New Testament. Genuine repentance and a life which reflects that change must not be separated. "Faith apart from works is dead (James 2:26). Jesus, speaking of his followers, said: "You will know them by their fruits" (Matt. 7:16). Often, we can be eager to be baptized for additional security but slow to turn from our sinful ways.

JOHN'S WITNESS TO JESUS (3:15-17)

John the Baptist's appearance in Judea awakened within the people the hope and dream that the Messiah's coming was approaching. Everything about John reminded the people of the prophets. Many began to wonder whether or not John himself might be the expected Messiah (v. 15). The Baptist quickly silenced the rumors about himself and pointed instead to the exalted One who soon would appear. Luke had said earlier that John was "the voice of one crying in the wilderness." (v. 4). The Gospel of John indicates that this interpretation originated from the Baptist himself (John l: 23). "The message was more than the messenger," declares Alfred Plummer, and hence the messenger Is regarded as mainly a voice."[8] Although some had hoped that this strange preacher of repentance might be the Christ, their expectations only revealed how vague their conceptions of the Messiah really were. Later some of the people, after John had been killed, would wonder if Jesus might be John the Baptist come back to life (9:19).

John denied emphatically that he was the Christ. He declared that the Messiah's mission was so much greater than his own. Untying sandals was the lowly work of a slave, yet John felt himself unworthy to do this service for the Messiah (v. 16). John distinguished his ministry from the Messiah's in two ways. First, he baptized only with "water." The Messiah would baptize with the Holy Spirit and fire." The Messiah would bring into reality what the Baptist had been able only to symbolize with water. Scholars are uncertain as to the exact meaning of the phrase "Holy Spirit and fire." It is probably a reference to the purifying activity of God within his people. The "Holy Spirit" refers to God's creative power to change people. Fire" symbolized purification and judgment. These are probably not two aspects but one part of the spirit's refining process. The Messiah was to be "like a refiner's fire" (Mal. 3:1-3).

Second, John the Baptist would proclaim the coming judgment of God and call for repentance. The Messiah would execute this judgment. John used an image from primitive threshing procedures to illustrate God's judgment. The winnowing fork was a large flat wooden shovel-like tool. The fork was used to toss the grain into the air. The heavy grain would fall to the ground in the process and the chaff was blown away by the wind. God's judgment, John declared, would separate the genuine believers and the unbelievers.

After the threshing process is completed. the farmers would dispose of the chaff by burning it. "Burn with unquenchable fire" refers to a fire which is so fierce that it cannot be extinguished or

---

8   Alfred Plummer, "The Gospel According to Luke," *The International Critical Commentary* (Edinburgh: T. & T. Clark, 1956), 86.

controlled. This judgment will be a time of separation. The Messiah will come in redeeming power for the faithful and in inescapable judgment on the disobedient. His judgment will either purify or consume. John's preaching was the voice calling for the people to get ready for the Christ who was coming.

Several decades before John began his ministry, a type of literature called apocalyptic (conveying a revelation) writings arose among the Jewish people. These people, who had long been oppressed, began to write in striking poetry their vision of the Messiah who was to liberate them. One example of this expression can be found in The Psalm of Solomon 17:23-25: "Behold, 0 Lord, and raise up unto them their king, the son of David, at the time in which thou seest, 0 God, that he may rule over Israel Thy servant. And gird him with strength, that he may shatter unrighteous rulers, and that he may purge Jerusalem from nations that trample (her) down to destruction. Wisely, righteously he shall thrust our sinners from (the) inheritance. He shall destroy the pride of the sinner as a potter's vessel. With a rod of iron, he shall break in pieces all their substance. He shall destroy the godless nations with word of his mouth." This may have been the image of the coming Christ which John had in his mind. When the ministry of Jesus did not fit this violent and political vision, that may have aroused John's puzzlement later which led him to inquire of Jesus "Are you he who is to come, or shall we look for another" (Matt. 11:3)?

THE MESSIAH AUTHENTICATED (3:21-22)

The baptism of Jesus by John the Baptist has continued to be a source of difficulty for the Christian Church. For Jesus to have been baptized by John was cited as evidence by some of the baptizer's followers that John was superior to Jesus. The Gospel writers obviously were aware of this teaching and had carefully demonstrated that John's role was one of preparation for Jesus. To show this, they had even quoted the words of John himself when he claimed that his role was secondary (vv. 15-16). Mark's account likewise shows John pointing beyond himself to the One mightier than he (Mark 1:7-8).

Matthew presents John as baptizing Jesus with reluctance (Matt. 3:14--15). The Gospel of John does not refer to it at all. Luke mentions Jesus' baptism after John has already been put in jail and without alluding to John regarding the baptism. John's baptism was administered to those who confessed and repented of their sins to make preparation for the Messiah's coming. If John's baptism was a baptism for the repentance of sins, why was Jesus baptized? The testimony of the New Testament affirms that Jesus was without sin. (Read 2 Cor. 5:21; Heb. 7:26; I Peter 2:22; I John 3:5). Why, then, did he, the Son of God, come to be baptized? Luke did not offer any explicit explanation as to why Jesus was baptized. (See Matt. 3:15). By implication, Luke may be offering some suggestions.

Luke linked the baptism of Jesus with that of the people. By his baptism, Jesus identified himself with his people who were sinners. He was not baptized because of his own sins, but for the sake of the people with whom he identified. Jesus, though sinless, took his place among the sinners for whom he had come to give his life. Isaiah 53 had depicted a "suffering servant," and Jesus identified here with the sinful humanity he had come to save. At the first public appearance of Jesus, Luke clearly noted the ultimate role which Jesus would assume as the ''suffering servant" (Phil. 2:8).

There is no question that all the Gospels show that the baptism of Jesus was the ending of his years of preparation in Nazareth and marked the beginning of his messianic mission. Luke, as a skilled historian, concluded the story of John the Baptist, and used the baptism scene as the inauguration of the public ministry of Jesus. He did not describe John's role in it because that is incidental now. The forerunner has completed his work and the stage was set for the appearance of the Christ.

Luke was the only one of the Gospel writers to mention that Jesus was praying at the time of his baptism. Baptism was not merely a form for him but a time of great spiritual crisis as Jesus identified with sinful humanity. It is at his baptism that Luke recorded God's witness to Jesus as the Christ. Most probably what happened was a personal experience to Jesus, but it came to him in answer to prayer. And it came as a voice of revelation and authentication. By identifying himself with sinners in the act of baptism, he received divine approval. Yes, to be my Son, you must walk the path of the suffering servant. "Thou art my beloved Son; with thee I am well pleased." The saying is composed of two Old Testament passages. The first half echoes Psalm 2:7 and the latter Isaiah 42:1. Jesus seemed to understand his role as it focused on his relationship to God as his Father. This was seen earlier in Jesus' visit to the temple as a lad of twelve (2:49), and now again at his baptism. He perceived of himself as God's son in a unique way from other men.

Some scholars believe that "beloved" is a messianic title, and this verse should read: "You are my Son, the Messiah." "With thee I am well pleased" is taken from Isaiah 42:1 which is a part of the suffering servant passages that culminates in Isaiah 52. In this experience, Jesus clearly perceived that he was the Messiah, God's Son in a "special" sense, but that this unique relationship would end in suffering and death. The descent of the Spirit in bodily form and the affirming voice of the Father put God's stamp of approval on Jesus and what he was beginning. According to the rabbis, the voice of God was the ultimate authority. The passage does not make it clear whether anyone else heard the voice or not, but probably it was heard only by Jesus.

At the baptism of Jesus, as he began his ministry, notice that all of the persons of the Trinity are mentioned, the Father, Son, and the Holy Spirit. This relationship is still a mystery to us, but it undergirded the work of Jesus from the moment of its commencement. During the years in Nazareth, Jesus must have struggled to understand his role in God's plan. At his baptism, Jesus received God's approval and his direction for ministry. In his genealogy (3:23-38), Luke was seeking to show that Jesus was not just the Savior for the Jewish people, but for all the human race. In keeping with the universal nature of his gospel, Luke did not end his line with Abraham, the father of the Jewish nation, but traced it back to Adam, the father of the human family.

Luke has not finished laying his background. He started at the birth of Jesus and traced his lineage back to the beginning of history. He mentioned the childhood of Jesus briefly. He has established the historical setting for the beginning of Jesus' ministry and the role of John the Baptist. The public ministry of Jesus was almost ready to begin, but first Jesus would draw apart for a time of solitude and prayer.

GRACE FOR SINNERS
Luke 5: 1-32

"You're known by the company you keep" is a familiar proverb. "Birds of a feather flock together" and "live with the wolves and you'll learn to howl" express a similar attitude. Most of us were taught while we were young to select our friends carefully. Our parents knew the power of peer pressure upon us. If you are a parent, you know how eagerly you longed for your children to choose friends who had high ethical and moral standards. We have always wanted our children to associate with Christian friends, and most of us have done the same.

Is this wrong? No, of course, it is not! As Christians, we need all the strength and support we can get from our friends. Their example and encouragement enable us to live a more effective life for Christ in an age when we are assaulted on every level with pagan expectations. But this very attitude, from which we draw strength, may often be the reason that we as Christians have difficulty in understanding why Jesus showed such concern and compassion for the "down and outs" and the known reprobates.

One of the most distinctive emphases of Luke's Gospel is the concern for the poor, the disadvantaged, and the sinful. In a series of recorded incidents, Luke showed how Jesus crossed the barriers separating sinners from the religious establishment and offered them forgiveness of sin and acceptance with God. Having been rejected by his own townspeople, Jesus carried the good news to those who felt they were unworthy of it. Jesus reached out and freed a man locked in by the forces of evil {4:31-37}. Jesus accepted and called a self-confessed sinner to be one of his disciples. "Depart from me, for I am a sinful man, Lord" (5:8). Then Jesus reached out, touched, and healed one of the most unacceptable of all society in his day, a leper. The only thing considered more defiled than a leper was a dead body. Jesus touched the untouchable (5:12-13)! Luke has placed these stories here to validate Jesus' claim as the Messiah. The story of healing the leper would certainly be a strong factor in his case. According to rabbinical teaching, the healing of a leper was almost as unlikely as raising the dead. He was regarded as hopeless and considered dead. And yet, with only a touch and a word, Jesus had cured a man of this most dreaded disease. Our focal passage now looks at two other incidents for specific study.

REDEMPTION FOR THE WHOLE PERSON (5:17-24)

Luke was not able to nail down the time of this story very well. He simply noted that it occurred "on one of those days" (v. 17) while Jesus was teaching in Galilee. Mark noted the place as Capernaum and stated that the miracle happened while Jesus was "at home" (Mark 2:1). This was probably the home of Peter and Andrew which was mentioned earlier (4:38-39). Jesus seemed to use it for a while as his base for teaching and healing. Earlier Jesus had cured Peter's mother-in-law of a severe fever (4:39). This, by the way, is undeniable evidence that Peter was married. Later the Apostle Paul referred to Peter's wife as his travelling companion (1 Cor. 9:5). Mark's account is more detailed because he most likely got the story from Peter himself.

The incident is a dramatic record of the faith of one man and his loyal friends. Jesus was teaching inside the house which was so full that the people had spilled out into the yard. The doorway and windows were so jammed with people that it was impossible to get inside. The paralytic's friends could have easily said to him: "Look, friend, it's impossible to see Jesus today! Look at this mob. Come on, let's go home. Maybe we can catch him when there are not so many people around." His four friends (Mark 2:3 gives us the number) however, are not discouraged so quickly. They

Sharing the Good News

located the outside staircase which led them to the roof of the house. The "bed" they were bringing the man on was more like a "mat," stretcher, or pallet. It is difficult to understand Luke's reference to '*tiles" (v. 19) since they were used on Roman houses and not in Palestine. They dug through the roof, which was probably constructed out of mud and branches, and made a hole to lower the pad through with the man on it into the presence of Jesus.

Try to imagine the commotions these men must have been making on the roof while Jesus was teaching below. The crowd must have wondered what was going on. Everything probably stopped for a few minutes until the enthusiastic friends had finished ripping open a hole and gently let their friend down to Jesus. People must have been shocked at the daring feat of these men. Luke indicated that Jesus himself must have been pleased. "When he saw their faith" (v. 20) includes a reference not only to the faith of the four men but most likely to the paralytic's faith as well. There is no way of knowing who was doing the most urging during this time. The paralytic certainly had some wonderful friends. They may have been the victims of some abuse and hostility as they tried to make their way to the Master.

If the people were shocked at the audacity of the men in breaking up the roof over their heads, they doubtlessly were even more shocked by what Jesus said and did. Jesus must have been moved by their act of faith, and immediately he said to the man: ''man, your sins are forgiven you" (v. 20). Mark had expressed the greeting with more affection, "son" or "child," while Matthew had prefaced his with "cheer up." Some scholars believe that the paralytic may have been a young man. This might have been a factor in their determination to see Jesus.

The verb is a form of the perfect tense, "have been forgiven." Jesus stated the forgiveness as an accomplished fact then. His sins had been forgiven, dismissed, or sent away. These words of Jesus did not necessarily indicate that this man's sins had caused his paralysis. They may have been the cause of his illness, or they may not have had any connection. Nevertheless, the paralyzed man may have believed that his ailment was a direct result of his own sinfulness. Jesus may have sensed that the man had to have the assurance of forgiveness before healing could take place. Sin may have been the man's deep-rooted problem. Many Jewish rabbis did teach that there was a close connection between sickness and sin. A commonly accepted view was that a sick man could not be well until his sins were forgiven. Jesus obviously did not accept this view. Read John 9:1-5. He certainly had to perform his ministry, however within the world view and understanding of his own day and age.

This may be a case in point. On the other hand, there are some maladies which may be the direct result of wanton sinfulness. The paralyzed man's illness might have been the consequence of his past sin. Whatever was the case, Jesus set him free with his forgiveness. If we had been present in the crowd then, we probably could have heard the gasp as the people could not believe their ears. Among those in this crowd there were present some Pharisees and teachers of the law from both Galilee and Judea. These were the religious leaders who were known as "the separated ones." They had committed their lives to living within the rules and regulations of their Oral Law. They were the Jewish legal experts. This group considered Jesus a law breaker, and they were constantly testing his orthodoxy. These men must have been visibly shaken and began to demand: "Who is this that speaks blasphemies? Who can forgive sins but God alone?" (v. 21). To them this was clearly an act of blasphemy.

Forgiveness of sins they believed was the prerogative which only God could possess. Blasphemy was punishable by death. Luke had now opened the door to see deeper into who Jesus really was. He had come not just to heal the physical needs of man. He had come to bring a deeper healing, within the heart of man. Here was the place where healing, wholeness, redemption took place. Luke wanted his readers to see that the primary authority of Jesus came in his ability to forgive sins. Luke was beginning to reveal that this man was far greater than any political messianic ideal they may have dreamed. Jesus, perceiving the questions and accusations, responded with a puzzling question of his own. The Pharisees' own theology taught "without forgiveness, there is no healing." "Which is easier, to say," Jesus asked them, "'Your sins are forgiven you,' or 'Rise and walk'?" (v. 23). No one could outwardly see the man's sins going away when they had been forgiven. But anybody would be able to see it if the man got up from his pallet and walked away.

Jesus then declared that he would perform an act that would give visible evidence that he did indeed have the right to forgive sins. "'But that you may know that the Son of man has authority on earth to forgive sins...rise, take up your bed and go home'" (v. 24). The man immediately did as Jesus had commanded. Luke alone among the gospel writers tells us that the man left "glorifying God." Luke records that they were "all" filled with these emotions: amazement, awe or fear, and gratitude. The "all" must have included the Pharisees and scribes as well. In this event, Luke has given us another indirect answer to the question, who is Jesus?

For the first time in Luke's Gospel, Jesus used the expression "Son of man" to describe himself. This was Jesus' favorite term for himself. He used it more than eighty times in the Gospels. In the Old Testament this term is found in at least three different books. Read Daniel 7:13-14, Ezekiel 2:1-3, 3:1-4 (and ninety other places), and Psalm 8:4. The image was a figure who was both mysterious and ambiguous. Sometimes it was used in a personal sense and on other occasions in a national sense. In Palestine the title commonly was used to mean "man" or "ideal man." Jesus may have used this title because it was ambiguous to his hearers. Throughout his ministry he did not publicly refer to himself as Messiah. Read 9:21 "Tell no one," and John 6:15. Jesus used the title in a significant way by adding the definite article "the Son of man." Jesus saw himself as fulfilling the Old Testament image of the "heavenly man" or "ideal man" of Daniel and Ezekiel's vision. For him, it was a messianic title.

CALLING A TAX COLLECTOR (5:27-28)

The tax collectors were considered on the level of the harlots as the dregs of Hebrew society. They were openly hated and despised by the rest of the people. The Roman government set an amount of tax money for each unit in the Empire. Taxes were then farmed out to the collectors. The Romans had to have their set amount, but they did not concern themselves with what they collected in addition. Unscrupulous collectors got rich gouging the poor and extorting unreasonable amounts from them. The Jewish people believed that no decent person would be a tax collector. They were despised because they worked for an alien government and made their profit by greed and graft as they sold out their own countrymen. Since they had chosen to flaunt the laws of God and the conventions of their own people, they were ostracized and avoided by decent people. Many called them the "dirty dogs" of society. The synagogue would not accept them. They were considered unfit for the company of respectable, God-fearing people. Many believed that they were traitors both to God and country.

For Jesus to call Levi as one of his disciples was a daring act. He was reaching out to one of the most despised and outcast of society and saying to him, "You, too can find forgiveness and newness of life. Come follow me." In calling Levi, Jesus knowingly risked the disapproval of the Pharisees. It is uncertain whether Jesus had talked with Levi before his call. There is no record of it. Most likely, though, he along with others had heard Jesus teach and may have been a part of the group that witnessed many miracles in the house of Simon Peter, including the paralyzed man. "After this he went out" does not necessarily mean the same day. Levi's "tax office" was most likely a booth where he sat collecting custom truces on commerce that moved through Galilee en route to various markets. Capernaum was located on one of the great trade routes of that day. Most scholars believe that Levi and Matthew are two names for the same apostle. Like Simon whose name became Peter when he followed Christ, Levi's name may have been changed to Matthew later. When Jesus came by and said, "Follow me," Levi left all to follow Jesus.

Where would Jesus go today to extend his call to the outcast of society? Who do you see as the publicans or sinners today? Jesus had identified with the wrong crowd then. Where would he see the greatest areas of need today? What does he want his Church, his followers to do about the sinners of the world who are often rejected by proper society?

Eating with Sinners (5:29-32)

Levi was so excited about his new commitment to Jesus that he invited his friends to share a banquet with Jesus as the honored guest. The "large company" would imply that Levi had the wealth to accommodate a large feast. The Pharisees, who would certainly not be eating at this table since they considered all the tax collectors ritually unclean, were probably standing nearby and criticizing. The crowd was so large that part of them, including some of the disciples, were likely being served in an open court of Levi's house. So, they could see them and even talk to them. The word "murmured" is a picturesque one according to A. T. Robertson. "It is like the buzzing of bees."[9] Levi had made his commitment and was willing to show the courage of his convictions.

But he and Jesus were quickly made the targets of criticism. They could not think less of him, so Jesus and his disciples were confronted. The Pharisees were shocked and enraged that a rabbi should demean himself by eating with publicans and sinners. They expressed their reproach and dismay to Jesus' disciples. Luke did not relate whether the disciples of Jesus tried to justify their teacher's actions. Jesus himself responded: "Those who are well have no need of a physician, but those who are sick; I have not come to call the righteous, but sinners to repentance" (vv. 31-32). A doctor does not avoid sick people when they need his medical help lest he become infected, Jesus was saying, but he attends to their mal-

---

9 A. T. Robertson, *Word Pictures in the New Testament*, Volume II (Nashville: Broadman Press, 1930), 77.

adies. As the Great Physician, Jesus had come to heal those who knew that they were spiritually ill. He saw that his ministry was to the sinners, just as a physician's work is directed to the physically sick. The Pharisees were concerned with being righteous by separating themselves from those they believed were unclean, like the tax-collectors and any others who could not observe their rituals. The Scribes and Pharisees did not seek out sinners. Rabbis would welcome a sinner in his repentance if he came on his initiative, but they would never go seek him out. C. G. Montefiore is convinced that the daring method of Jesus in seeking the sinner instead of avoiding his bad company was "something new in the religious history of Israel."[10]

Jesus' purpose with sinners and the outcast was not to become like them and lower his standards to theirs. The phrase "to repentance" is recorded only by Luke. Jesus does indeed call sinners while they are in their sin, but this is to call them out of it. He was willing to go wherever he was needed the most. Labels and barriers did not stop him; he crossed them to reach those in need. Jesus did not come to call "the righteous." They would have no need of a Savior. This was said, of course, ironically in reference to the Pharisees. They only thought they were righteous. They, too, were sinners in need of a Savior.

One of Luke's central emphases has been to show the universality of the gospel. Jesus Christ had come to be the Savior of the whole world. Early in his Gospel, Luke observed in Simeon's song that Jesus was "a light…to the Gentiles" (2:32). In the last words of Jesus to his disciples, he instructed them to preach in his name "to all nations" (24:47). The large emphasis on the ministry to Samaritans was another way Luke had of stressing the universal nature of the gospel that crossed all classes, races, and barriers (9:51- 56; 10:25-37; 17:11-19). As the Savior of the world, Luke showed the concern Jesus had with those who were the outcast and lost ones in society. Several of the parables,

---

10   C. G. Montefiore, *Some Elements of the Religious Teaching of Jesus* (London: MacMillan and Co., 1910), 57.

unique to Luke, focus in this area: the Last Coin, the Lost Sheep, the Lost Son (15:1-32). and the Pharisee and the Publican (18:9-14). The story of Zacchaeus (19:1-10), the Pharisee and the sinful woman (7:36-50), and the forgiveness of the thief on the cross emphasized the loving concern of Jesus with sinful humanity.

The Church is the only institution in the world which meets weekly and acknowledges that it is composed of sinners. The Church is not for the righteous. All are sinners, some are sinners saved by grace, but still sinners. All are imperfect. Its doors are extended to other sinners, from all walks of life, to find healing and redemption in Jesus Christ. Our mission is to share the knowledge of this Christ with others. The same Lord who reached out to the poor, the sick, the outcast of his own day, has continued to extend his forgiving hand to sinful men and women through the centuries. Jesus has swept all barriers away as he calls sinners to repentance.

PUTTING PERSONS BEFORE TRADITIONS
Luke 5:33 to 6:11

For many, religion is more like a heavy burden to be borne, than a force which sustains, uplifts, and refreshes us. I remember a dear lady who was a strong influence on my early Christian thinking. She worked faithfully with our youth group and provided us with a model for our Christian faith. Unfortunately, her way of understanding Christianity was mostly negative. The Christian faith began to emerge as a religion which emphasized what "you don't do," "and never would you do," "you could not possibly do," and "On no occasion can you do." There are certainly things which a Christian wants to refrain from, but Christianity is not basically a negative way of life. Later I began to see that my Christian faith was not so much something I had to work at but an awareness that Christ was at work within me. The good news of the gospel is that we are saved by grace not by works. That does not mean that there are no responsibilities or demands. There are many. But we walk with a new sense of joy and a consciousness of a shared load. We travel no longer with the dead weight of our own sins and struggles but with the liberating strength of the one who said: "Come to me, all who labor and are heavy laden, and I will give you rest. Take my yoke upon you and learn from me; for I am gentle and lowly in heart, and you will find rest for your souls. For my yoke is easy, and my burden is light" (Matt. 11:28-30).

Religious tradition can be a strong factor in helping to mold the belief and practices of persons. To the Hebrew people, their strong sense of history and tradition enabled them to sustain their identity as a nation for almost four thousand years. Jesus himself followed faithfully many of these traditions. He had worshipped for years in Nazareth "as his custom was." He participated in many of the religious festivals with his disciples and made special preparation to observe his final Passover feast with them (Luke 22: 7-13). Yet, Jesus directed some of his harshest words against those who had turned sacred experiences and ideas into irrelevant entanglements and detailed concerns over trivialities. Professional religionists had distorted meaningful sacred tradition into trivial legalism and meaningless observances. The sabbath, which began as a beneficent institution for the Hebrew people, was twisted into an endless concern over the observance of meticulous rules.

The sabbath was the most important and distinctive institution of Judaism. Because the sabbath was so central in Judaism, numerous rules had been established by the religious leaders to help people know how to obey the Commandment. Read the commandment in Deut. 5:13-14. The sabbath Commandment had prohibited work. The rabbis believed that the kind of work which was forbidden by this Commandment needed to be specified carefully. In order to define what was work on the sabbath, the rabbis had drawn up a list of thirty-nine classes of activities which were unlawful. Under the interpretation of this law, minute distinctions were made such as a woman could wear a ribbon if it were sewed on her dress but not if it were merely pinned on. A ribbon which was pinned on was not secure enough to be worn on the sabbath. That would be carrying a burden. A woman could not use a mirror on the sabbath. The reasoning for this was that she might see a gray hair and pluck it out. That was reaping. These examples to us may seem humorous, but this kind of precise detail became a weight crushing the people under its load.[11]

---

11 Alfred Plummer, "The Gospel According to S. Luke," *The International Critical Commentary* (Edinburgh: T. & T. Clark, 1956), 168.

To ensure that no commandment be passed over, the rabbis claimed to have traced out the principles behind the laws of Moses. They had concluded that there were 613 commandments. 365 of these were negative and 248 were positive. To serve God each person had to try to live in accordance with this vast legal system. No wonder religion had become a dreary burden for many. The penalty for violating the sabbath was exclusion from the Jewish community (Ex. 31:14) or death by stoning (Num. 14:32-36). Violators were usually given one warning. The Violation of Sabbath Rules (6:1-2) As the hungry disciples of Jesus were going through a grain field on one sabbath day, they broke off some of the grain, rubbed the kernels between the palms of their hands, and then ate them. Luke alone records the process of "rubbing the grain." The Pharisees saw this act as a daring defiance of the law. It was, however, not the fourth commandment which they referred to, since it simply forbade "work." But the doctors of the law had defined "work" in their expansion of this commandment in hair-splitting details. On seeing this, the Pharisees accused them of breaking the sabbath law. They were not accosted for taking the grain, because the law allowed that act for the poor (Deut. 23:25). This also reveals how hard the times must have been for them on occasions.

According to the Pharisees, the disciples would have broken at least four kinds of sabbath rules: reaping, threshing, winnowing, and preparing food. The plucking of the grain was considered reaping. When they rubbed their hands until the grain was separated from the chaff, that was threshing. The chaff which they blew away after it was separated was winnowing. The whole action would have been looked upon as a meal preparation. To us today, this whole matter seems petty and almost unbelievable. To the Pharisees, who had committed their lives to the strict keeping of the law, this kind of activity was irreligious. It was certainly not what you would expect from the disciples of a rabbi. Jesus selects a precedent from the Scriptures (6:3-4) In a twist of irony, Jesus asked the men who had devoted their lives to pouring over the details of the law: "Have you not read..?" You who are supposed to be the experts in interpreting the minute concepts of the law, have you never read, studied, or understood the incident of King David and the priest of Nob? These guardians of orthodoxy had certainly read that passage many times but reading and understanding are two different things.

Read the record of this event in 1 Samuel 21:1-6. Jesus reminded them of the occasion when David was fleeing from Saul, and he and his men had no food to eat. David persuaded Ahimelech, the priest at Nob, to allow him and his hungry fugitives to eat the sacred bread which was forbidden by the law except for the priests (Lev. 24: 5-9). The bread David ate was the twelve "consecrated loaves" which were placed on a special table in the Holy Place of the temple every Sabbath. The bread of the presence came to be called "shew bread" later. David and his men had clearly violated sacred tradition and law.

The Pharisees had not labeled this act sinful because David was revered as the man after God's heart and the brightest light in their national history. Neither he nor his men had been condemned for an act which was a far greater violation of ceremonial law than the disciples plucking a few heads of grain. The "doctors of the law" had made an exception of David's action. Why? In this case they were willing to acknowledge that human need (David's hunger) took precedence over religious tradition.

The disciples had taken of their simple food for the same reason that David and his men ate the shewbread. They were hungry. Just as human need had justified David's violating the ritualistic law, so the hunger of the disciples took precedence over rigid sabbath observances. The Pharisees had permitted this on other occasions, why were they so quick to condemn such a simple act to satisfy a genuine human need?

One of the unfortunate things about this narrow approach to life is the rigid negativism it breeds into our perspective. When we begin to live primarily by a philosophy of "thou shall not," it colors our attitude toward ourselves and others. A negative perspective is usually a critical one. We begin to see mostly the faults of others and what is wrong with institutions like the church, the government, school, and others. We want others to see it our way or not at all. We soon become the modern-day version of the Pharisees who are more concerned about the letter of the law than the meaning or reason behind it. We may become more concerned with rules. rituals, and form than we do with persons and their needs. Think, for example, if you are asked to say something positive about someone, how many adjectives come to your mind? How many positive attributes leap into your mind? On the other hand, if you are asked to list the negative features, notice how much quicker they will often come to your mind. Why is it that we can usually think of more negative things about other people than we can positive ones? The roots of negativism seem to be buried deep within us. Only by the strong presence of the Christ within can we begin to see life differently. Like the Lord we serve, we need to strive to see the potential for the best in the very worst of people. We will not lift up anyone when we are constantly pulling that person down.

LORD OF THE SABBATH (6:5)

If the Pharisees had been amazed at Jesus' knowledge of and skill in the interpretation of the Scriptures, they must have been openly shocked at his declaration: "The Son of man is Lord of the sabbath." Again, Jesus avoided any use of the expression Messiah, but the implication seemed evident. Just as David had eaten of the sacred bread to meet his need, now the Son of David put aside ritualistic sabbath regulations to meet human need. His claim of Lordship over the sabbath was a declaration that the messianic age had begun. Since the Messiah will bring judgment when he initiates his kingdom, he has the right to supersede the sabbath law and not be controlled by it. In other words, Jesus reached behind the sabbath regulation to the very reason it was established and stated that he had authority to see that it was used properly.

The word "Lord" was used by Luke to describe who Jesus was and is. All three of the gospel writers stressed "Lord", and it is placed first in the Greek construction to show emphasis. Read the parallel passages in Mark 2:23-28 and Matthew 12:1-8. Mark added the phrase "the sabbath was made for man, not man for the sabbath" (Mark 2:27). Even some of the rabbis had already admitted this in earlier sayings like "The sabbath is handed over to you; not you are handed over to the sabbath." The sabbath day, instead of being a burden and a curse, was intended to be a day of rest and refreshment. In times of need, rules and laws must be superseded. Jesus, who was more than ordinary man, was the Son of man. As the messianic age was dawning in him, Jesus was not so much destroying the sabbath laws and other regulations but fulfilling them. (See Matthew 5:17-20.)

Because of their closed minds, the Pharisees could not see who Jesus was. They were astonished at his bold claim. Ernst Kasemann, in his book, *Jesus Means Freedom*, declares that this is the most scandalous saying Jesus ever made.[12] The attitude which Jesus expressed here was the primary factor which later led to his crucifixion. It is difficult for us to realize how deeply Jesus' words and actions cut into the religious system of his day. Like a razor Jesus cut through decades of religious observances and challenged persons to live on a deeper level of love and mercy. At stake here was a way of life. To the Pharisees, rules and regulations came first. Often men and women were enslaved and depersonalized by these restrictions. Unfortunately, by setting such a hard and narrow line, they had made the means more important than the end. The externals of religion became more important than the end goal.

As "Lord of the sabbath" Jesus attempted to reverse that approach. He was more concerned with people and with the inner meaning of religion. The only interpretation of rules and regulations which are in keeping with God's purpose are those which make the urgency of human need central. In claiming to be "Lord

---

12   Ernst Kasemann, *Jesus Means Freedom* (London: SCM Press, 1969), 25.

of the sabbath," Jesus declared his authority to set aside any manmade rules in order to meet human need.[13]

A Sabbath Healing (6:6-10)

Sometime later, on another sabbath day, but not necessarily the next one, Jesus was teaching in a synagogue. Luke probably put both of these accounts together since they dealt with the same type of controversy. The law was clear. To heal on the sabbath day was forbidden except in cases where a life was endangered, or extreme circumstances called for emergency measures. In the synagogue where Jesus was teaching was a man with a withered hand. Pharisees were present and were watching him to see if he would heal the man and break the sabbath law.

The Pharisees had come for only one purpose, to spy upon Jesus. They "watched" indicates watching with sinister intentions. There did not appear to be any concern for the man with the paralyzed hand. In seeing a person with an affliction, there was no compassion for him and his difficulty but an obsession with upholding a rigid law. Rather than violate some abstract law. they believed that the man should remain crippled. His life was not threatened. This was obviously not an emergency. If Jesus wanted to heal the man, he could wait until the sabbath was over at six o'clock and then perform his act. "No, not before," they thought to themselves. "This man can wait. After all, he has been crippled for some time. Why should the sabbath law be violated just to cure him now?"

Jesus knew the sabbath restrictions, and his healing of the crippled man was obviously an act of defiance. He wanted to use this tense situation as an opportunity to teach the people. He would challenge the most sacred of all the Jewish traditions and demonstrate this time that he was "lord of the sabbath." Knowing their thoughts, Jesus asked the crippled man to come forward from his seat and stand where all there could see him. Jesus was not interested in doing something in secret, like the spying Phar-

---
13   William Manson, *The Gospel of Luke* (New York: Harper & Row, n.d.), 60.

isees. He wanted the man in a place where all eyes could witness what was going to happen.

This time he takes the initiative and puts the Pharisees on the defensive with his question: "I ask you, is it lawful on the sabbath to do good or to do harm, to save life or to destroy it?" No rabbi would acknowledge that the sabbath day was designed for people to do harm or evil. But Jesus said not to do good when there was an opportunity was evil in itself. This thought was expressed in a similar way in James 4:17, "Whoever knows what is right to do and fails to do it, for him it is sin." To see this man in need and to refuse to help him would be the same as doing evil.

Jesus may have also been pointing the idea even more directly at the Pharisees. Their evil intentions and plots against him on the sabbath may have made them the real violators of the sabbath and not Jesus. He was asking them, in effect, which way keeps the spirit of the sabbath better, his way of doing good or the Pharisees' way of plotting evil against him? The Pharisees had come "so they might find an accusation against him." His aim and motive were directed toward good; their intent was evil. Which is a better design for the use of the sabbath?

The scribes and Pharisees were silent (Mark 3:4). And well they might be! What response could they give without abandoning their rigidity and pride. They did not want to choose either of those two alternatives. And so, they remained silent. But in the absence of their non activity, Jesus acted. He commanded the man to "stretch out" his paralyzed hand. Was there someone present, who wanted to say to Jesus: "But, Master, you don't understand. That is the one thing he cannot do?" Only Luke, in his eye for details, related that it was the man's right hand. In the noncanonical *Gospel of the Nazarenes*, the crippled man is said to be a stonemason who implored Jesus: "Restore me my health that I may not shamefully beg for food." He obeyed the command of Jesus to do the impossible and in doing so, Jesus healed him. The very act of his willingness to follow this command indicated how great was his desire to be healed. Sometimes the word from Christ seems to be an impossible one to follow. But with his command goes the strength to realize that he has called us to accomplish. Only in the willingness to obey will we experience the power of his presence.

THE RESPONSE TO THE MIRACLE (6:11)

None of the Gospel writers recorded the response of the man or his family to the healing. They obviously were elated and probably went home praising God. But all three writers indicated that the scribes, Pharisees, and the Herodians (included by Mark 3:6) began to plan how they might "destroy him" (Matt. 12:13; Mark 3:6). Luke's phrase is not as harsh, "what they might do to Jesus," but it implied the same end for him. Luke noted that the Pharisees "were filled with fury." Robertson says that this is "rage that is kin to insanity."[14] Their anger was so intense that it filled them with "madness" or "lack of reason" or "folly." Their criticism turned to hatred and their fury into a plan to stop Jesus. Jesus had scandalized their most sacred day, the sabbath, and they felt he was deserving of the death penalty for this violation. Read Exodus 31:14.

Jesus had revealed that they were blind and heartless leaders, more concerned about traditions than persons. Although they could not refute Jesus, they planned how they might stop him. The sounds of "crucify, crucify him" were beginning to take shape. The Pharisees realized that they would have to do more than discredit Jesus, they could not rest until he was dead.

It is sad when anyone chooses to be proper or correct legally rather than good. Jesus challenged a "do-nothing" attitude on the sabbath. Jesus affirmed that it is always right to do good on the sabbath. Now his question turns toward us. What customs or traditions do you have that may keep you from serving Jesus more effectively where you live? In some areas community mores have replaced the principles of Jesus. Are we sometimes afraid to "rock the boat" and challenge the status quo in our society? Test

---
14 A. T. Robertson, *Word Pictures in The New Testament* (Nashville: Broadman Press, 1930) Volume II, 83.

the customs and traditions of your community by the principles Jesus mentioned in his response to the Pharisees. Do these traditions or customs demean or damage persons? Do they help or hurt persons? Does the gospel of Christ challenge us to change those things in our society which do not give persons first priority? The way of Jesus may not be easy, but we have the assurance of his presence and power.

The Radical Demand of Agape
Luke 6:12-49

Several years ago in Nelson County, Virginia, following a deluge of rainfall, a devastating flood swept through a part of that community late one night. Bridges were destroyed, houses were overturned, telephone poles were snapped off, and dozens of people were killed. The community looked like it had been in a war. And in a way, it had, with the forces of nature. Few had ever witnessed such power before. But it was uncontrolled power. It was power gone wild, without direction or purpose. There is a great deal of power in the world, both natural and human, but unless it is controlled, it may be destructive or wasteful.

Jesus was aware of the potential power within persons for good or evil. His call to discipleship was a summons to a radical new control over this power within. The primary motive governing all the disciples' living was to be love. The idea of love being the touchstone for all decision making and relating to self, others and God seemed to run counter to much in human nature. After all, many have said that self-preservation is nature's first law. But Jesus challenged that idea and placed love as the driving power in his disciples' lives. Love was made the basic motive and method of controlling one's life. It was indeed a radical demand.

JESUS CHOOSES HIS DISCIPLES (6:12-13)

With the hostility of the Pharisees now growing and their rejection of his teachings becoming more apparent on numerous occasions, Jesus went into the hills to plan his ministry. Luke alone among the Gospel writers tells us that Jesus prayed all night before he chose his twelve disciples. Luke recorded twelve occasions in which Jesus prayed. Luke gave great prominence to prayer. There are more references to prayer in Luke than in the other gospels. Luke alone recorded the importance of prayer at the baptism of Jesus (3:21), the calling of the twelve (6:12), the confession (9:18), the transfiguration (9:28), and Peter's denial (22:31-34). The power of prayer seemed to strengthen Jesus to endure the horrible ordeal of the cross. He prayed as he faced crucifixion (22:42), as he was nailed to the cross (23:34), and in his very moment of dying (23:40). Several of Jesus' parables also noted the importance of prayer (11:5-8; 18:1-8; 9-14).

Prayer seemed to provide for Jesus a source of unparalleled power. In his times alone with his Father, Jesus attained guidance for his own ministry and the role his disciples would have. Jesus probably had a large group of followers, and he now had to decide which ones would make up the inner circle. Can we imagine how he must have lifted name after name up in prayer, as he made his decision. This time, as he did on so many other occasions, Jesus emerged from his night of solitude refreshed and his decisions clearly made.

The next morning Jesus gathered his disciples (the learners) together and announced the twelve whom he had selected from the larger group of his followers. The number twelve was probably symbolic of the twelve tribes of Israel (22:30). This group of twelve represented the "New Israel." Luke called the twelve "apostles" which means "someone who is sent out." An apostle was someone sent as a representative by another to act under the authority of his name. To indicate the seriousness of this selection, Jesus said to them: "He who hears you hears me, and he who rejects you rejects him who sent me" (10:16). Although Luke used the designation apostle to describe the twelve, Matthew and Mark use that term only once each (Matt. 10:2; Mark 6:30). Read Acts 2;21-23 for Luke's further word about the apostle who replaced Judas Iscariot. The key role of the apostles can be stated in the following summary: (1) They became the inner circle of Jesus' friends. He chose them "that they might be with him" (Mark 3:14). (2) Jesus devoted much time to teaching, training, and commissioning them to preach. (3) They played a central role in the story of the Gospels. (4) The gospel accounts rest on the witness of the apostles. When the early church was seeking to determine which writings were canonical, they chose ones related directly or indirectly to an apostle. (5) The twelve were ordinary men with no special education for this kind of ministry. Yet, from this group the New Israel was formed which would become God's missionary force to the nations.

A Hard Saying (6:27-31)

Scholars have debated at great length whether this account in Luke (often called the Sermon on the Plain) and Matthew's record of the Sermon on the Mount {Matthew 5-7) are the same discourse or two different sermons. The more likely truth is that they are the same. Each writer probably selected much of the same material and arranged it topically and theologically to meet the emphasis of his Gospel. After Jesus had selected his disciples, he descended to a level place (the word is "level place" not "a plain") on the mountainside where the multitude of people were gathered and began to teach them. First, Jesus presented the "blessing" (Beatitudes) and woes that would mark the character of his disciples. The rest of the sermon focused on the inner law of love as the essence of his disciples' true character.

The teaching of Jesus in vv. 27-30 is regarded by most scholars as among the most difficult sayings of Jesus and one of the hardest to fulfill. Friedrich Nietzsche, a German philosopher, called this passage an indication of the slave morality of the Christian faith.

But Jesus did not utter these words out of cowardice or fear. He was giving to his followers a direction for living which was to be a way of overcoming force and brutality. In the Graeco-Roman world, the supreme virtue was courage. The ability to stand up to one's enemies and best them in encounters were the marks of the hero. The story of Odysseus slaying the suitors of Penelope without mercy was the idea of heroism in that ancient day.

In place of revenge and retaliation, Jesus raised a higher standard: "Love your enemies." This must have sounded like a bitter lesson for the Jewish people. They were living in a country occupied and controlled by an enemy government. They longed for a Messiah who would throw off the Roman yoke and give them their freedom. In our native English language, we have only one word to express a variety of loves. We use the same word to express devotion to our wife or husband, parent, or child, to our country or to our God. We love Mom, but we also love ice cream. We love to read, swim, fish, cook, or wear old shoes. From the highest that we know to the most trivial, we use the same word to express our feelings. We are unfortunate in this respect because we cannot show any distinctions or exactness in our use of such a beautiful word.

The Greek language is much richer in this regard. They have four words to distinguish various kinds of love. *Storge* is affection between family members and near relatives (family love). *Philia* is close to our word for friendship. *Eros* is sexual love or desire. *Agape is* Christian love. It is a strong feeling of good will toward others. It is an attitude dependent on will not sentiment. All of these various Greek words are used in the New Testament with the exception of *Eros*.

Love in this verse is in the imperative. But can love be commanded? It cannot be commanded if it is merely sentiment or emotion, like "falling in love." The love which Jesus is speaking about here is *agape*. It is linked with a command because it is a matter of the will not emotions or sentiment. This command has nothing to do with romantic feelings or the attitude of the other person toward us. It is a sustained determination to show good will toward our enemies.

Loving your enemy does not mean that you even have to "like" him or her. Liking someone is based on a matter of feeling. Some people are difficult to like. No one has to approve of the actions of his enemies nor like their sinful behavior. But *agape* challenges the Christian to act toward others in the most helpful and creative way possible. Loving our enemies does mean that we seek to help them no matter what the cost or consequences may be to us. *Agape* is always self-sacrificing and self-giving. Jesus never said his way would be easy. It calls for strong determination to show good, even to those who would do us harm.

Agape is a determined interest in the true welfare of others. It is so strong that it cannot be stopped by hatred, cursing, or abuse. Christ's followers are not to come down to the level of their enemies but are to be like God in doing good to their enemies. Doing good to those who hate, blessing those who curse, and praying for those who abuse represent *agape*, undiscourageable goodwill in action (v. 28). In vv. 29-30, Jesus offered some illustrations of the principle which he had just stated. When a person is attacked the natural inclination is to strike back. The impulse is to meet evil with evil, force with force, or "an eye for an eye and a tooth for a tooth" (Matt. 5:38). Jesus suggested a new form or resistance which was so radical that it might disarm its advocate.

If a disciple receives a blow to the cheek (not just an insult but a heavy blow), how is he to respond? Jesus' answer is not just to stand there and take it but to use the occasion as an opportunity to teach an unexpected lesson by offering "the other also." The cloak was the outer garment and the coat the inner garment. If someone takes your outer garment, give him the undergarment as well. Jesus said be generous to beggars, and if someone takes your goods, don't ask him to return them. Christ's followers are to be generous and limitless in their concern for the needs of others. Jesus pictured insult and injury, personal violence and robbery, abuse, and theft. He called upon his followers to meet this kind of evil not with what would be expected but with active goodwill (agape). To fight evil on its terms, Jesus believed, was to surrender to it. Insult, injury, and hatred are not overcome by returning what one receives. Immoral means do not accomplish moral ends. Love (agape) alone can transform them.

The *Agape* demands of love are hard. You are probably asking if it is always helpful to another person to give in to all his demands. Is there no responsibility to help sinners change? Did Jesus mean for his followers to take this literally? Can we afford to practice this ethic in a dog-eat-dog world? These questions have troubled believers of all ages. If we are to practice this ethic in the world, how can we change from hostile and resentful people into agape-type persons? How can this command impact business and corporate action? Jesus knew that this message did not give the whole of his teaching. At this stage, however, his disciples needed to be freed from their own self-centeredness and concern for their own selfish ends. He wanted to focus their attention on meeting the needs of others. He began with the most extreme case, their enemies. If his followers could begin to love them, then truly God's power had entered their lives.

The Golden Rule (v. 31), "And as you wish that persons would do to you, do so to them," has its parallels in many religious cultures. It is found in Judaism, for example, in Tobit 4:14: "And what you hate, do not do to anyone." The Stoics had a similar saying: "What you do not wish done to you, do not to another." But in all these cultures the precept is expressed in a negative way. Jesus stated this maxim in a positive way and gave it a deeper perspective. The command of Jesus is not simply to refrain from some kind of actions but actively to seek to do good things toward others. This verse, as a summary of the teachings of Jesus, challenges self-interest and directs the Christian to live in an unlimited benevolent way. In our dealings with others, we must be guided by the principle of love (*agape*). We learn to do this by putting ourselves in the place of others and asking what we would like done to us in that situation. If this were done more frequently, imagine the difference it would make in all walks of life.

LIVING ABOVE SELF-INTEREST (6:32-36)

The nature of *agape* love does not depend on whether someone is able to reciprocate. This love goes out of its way, just as God's love does for us, to assist others. It takes no special grace or effort to love those who love us, to do good to those who reciprocate, and to lend to those who pay us back and return the favor if we need a loan. Pagans or atheists can function on this level. Jesus challenged his followers to live on a higher level than this. The word "credit" is a translation of the beautiful Greek word for grace. Grace is God's undeserved favor which he has given to people. Just as his followers have experienced grace, which was not earned or deserved, they in turn should express grace to those who are unloving, difficult, hostile or even their enemies.

To love one's enemies, the ungrateful, and selfish is to be filled with "grace." This kind of love is not acting because it is attracted to these people, nor expects something in response but loves in order to help the other person. Love is not concerned about boundaries or restraints but reaches out spontaneously because there is an opportunity and a need. *Agape* labors without looking for recognition or reward. Several years ago, in a church where I was pastor, one of our fine ladies took upon herself the responsibility of looking after an elderly woman in the congregation who had no family to assist her. This lady was very generous with her time and attention. She bought groceries each week for her, baked cakes, and pies for her, and stopped by often just to talk with her and check on her. Unfortunately, the elderly lady was a very grouchy, crabby, and pettish individual that no one could really satisfy very well. One day, the woman's husband asked her, "Why in the world do you fool with Mrs. Blank? She doesn't appreciate anything you do for her." "No, she doesn't," the Christian lady responded. "But I don't do it to be appreciated." That was the spirit of agape. She helped because there was a need, and she did not look for compensation. To serve in the Master's name is enough.

The statement about Christians not lending money for interest was taken quite literally by the early Christians.[15] The loaning of money soon became a business of the Jews and, unfortunately, added greatly to the harsh attitude which many Christians had toward them. "Your reward will be great, and you will be sons of the Most High" (v. 35). The reward for the radical demand of Jesus to love one's enemies is an appeal to the highest kind of personal motive. The reward for this action was not announced as fame, wealth, status, success, recognition, or even acceptance by others. The reward for serving in such a difficult capacity will be fellowship with God. Once again Jesus urged his followers to "love your enemies, and this time he assured them that to do so they would "be sons or daughters of the Most High."

How different Jesus' challenge is for walking in his way than some of the cheap and easy appeals which are often heard today. Some invite us to follow Jesus so we might become rich, or famous, or slim, or sexier. Jesus invites us to accept no cheap grace but God's grace of undeserved love which will give us fellowship with him as his son or daughter. Jesus called his followers to shape their conduct after God who is kind to "the ungrateful and selfish." The "lovingkindness" of God motivates us to serve him. Those who are the "sons of the Most High" should imitate him in their conduct. The true children of God will be merciful toward others as God is merciful to us all. To love like God indicates that we are indeed his child. "To be merciful" might not seem to be as strong as Matthew's injunction "to be perfect" (5:48) but both carry the meaning of striving to be like "your Father." Luke's phrase "your father" (v.36) carries with it a strong identification with God. As his son or daughter, we have identified with him to live in his merciful way-- Letting God Be the Judge (6:37-38). The saying on judgment is a natural outworking of the principle of love. "Judge

---

15 Alfred Plummer, "The Gospel According to St. Luke," *The International Critical Commentary* (Edinburgh: T. & T. Clark, 1956), 188.

not" because only God can be the true judge. God alone knows what a person thinks, what his circumstances really are like, what influences, and pressures have molded him. If God, in his mercy, has forgiven us, then the Christian is grateful for this grace and should not in turn sit in judgment upon another.

If the Christian has no right to vengeance, he or she has even less right to judge. "Good measure, pressed down, shaken together, running over" (v. 38) is an image drawn from the grain market. It simply refers to filling a container until it is full and overflows at the top. The word "lap" was a sort of a big pocket which could be formed in the robe by drawing it up into a deep fold above the girdle for carrying things. This figure indicates the overflowing experience with God's bounty when the Christian is open and responsive to God and allows God's grace to reach others through him instead of trying to contain him.

The rule of measure for measure is not a "tit for tat" approach. The teaching that a person must forgive if he is to be forgiven is found in many of the sayings of Jesus (Read Mark 11:25; Matt. 6:14-15). The emphasis is not on bargaining with God, but on "the principle that God's gifts come only to those through whom they can find an outlet to others."[16] Thus, the believer does not forgive in order to receive but because he has already been forgiven and has received God's blessings. The unforgiving person is himself unforgiven because in closing the door to another, he or she closes it on himself or herself. The generous person knows forgiveness because he is forgiving and God's grace flows through him to others. For it is in giving that we receive; it is in spending ourselves in service that we save; and it is by losing ourselves in ministry for others that we find ourselves.

---

16 William Manson, *The Gospel of Luke* (New York: Harper & Brothers, n.d.), 71.

The Sweep of Christ's Love
Luke 7:1-50

A small boy who had witnessed a young woman almost drown was expressing his frustration to his father. "Daddy," he sighed, "People were all up and down the beach. They heard her cries and saw that she needed help. But none went to help her. Finally, a man on the street, who was simply walking by heard her screams and came to her rescue. The rest just didn't seem to care." "It may seem like that," the father responded, "But don't judge them too harshly, son. Remember, it takes great courage to care."

Caring is a powerful emotion. Unfortunately, everyone has not always wanted to express it. In the first century the philosophy of Stoicism was very strong. Adherents to this thinking tried to suppress their feelings. The stronger individuals would not show any emotions such as anger, joy, sorrow, or pain. That would be a sign of weakness. God, according to this philosophy, was incapable of feeling. If God could be influenced by others, this would make them superior to him. God was noted for his apathy or lack of feeling. Into this apathetic climate Jesus came. Instead of being unsusceptible, he was deeply moved by the needs of those around him. Instead of a God of unconcern, Jesus revealed that his Father cared so much for the world that he sent his only Son (John 3:16).

This chapter in Luke focuses on two incidents from Jesus' ministry to show how his love reached out to all kinds of people. Luke put special emphasis on the concern Jesus expressed for the sick. the sorrowing, the helpless, and the outcast of society. Keep in mind as we look at these two stories the earlier account of the

Roman centurion's slave whom Jesus healed. The fact that he was a Gentile indicated the universal nature of Jesus' concern which would break down all barriers of race and nations (7:1-10).

A Condition of Utter Desolation (7:11-12)

Luke alone recounts this story. Scholars are uncertain as to the location of "Nain." Most locate it as the modern Nein, a small town about eight miles southwest of Nazareth, and near Shunem where Elisha had performed a similar miracle. See 2 Kings 4:21-37. In Jesus' travels now he was accompanied by not only his disciples but also a great crowd. As he approached the city of Nain, he met a funeral procession on its way to the cemetery outside the city. In biblical times professional mourners were often a part of the funeral procession. But in this particular case, the mourners are identified as townspeople--"a large crowd from the city." Since this woman was a widow and this was her only son, they were probably friends deeply concerned for her.

The loss of a son at any time would have been grievous under any circumstance, but in the first century setting, she was in desperate trouble. Women held a status like that of minors in today's society. They could not inherit property, and they were dependent on men for both protection and provision. Without a man to care for her, a woman was defenseless. In losing her only son, the widow would have to hope for charity from someone in her husband's family.

One of the special emphases of Luke was to show Jesus' high regard and concern for women. In the early chapters dealing with the birth stories, Luke focused on Mary and Elizabeth. He alone mentioned Anna, the aged prophetess in the temple (2:36-50). It is only Luke who told the accounts of the widow at Nain, the penitent women in Simon's house (7:36-50), the women who ministered to Jesus (8:1-3), the visit to the home of Mary and Martha (10: 38-42), the healing of the crippled woman (13:10-17), and the two parables in which women are the central figures (15:8-10; 18:1-8). This again was part of Luke's universal emphasis. The Apostle Paul stated the universal nature of God's salvation in Christ where "there is neither male nor female" (Gal. 3: 28). When Jesus saw this woman. "he had compassion on her." This is the strongest word in Greek to express pity and sympathy. This strong word was used several times by Matthew and Mark, but this is the only place where Luke records it. Jesus was moved deeply because of her loss. Out of his deep compassion, he spoke a word of hope to her. "Do not weep." This verb indicates that the woman was weeping at the present time and Jesus told her: "Do not go on weeping."

The woman was probably shocked by all this. It is most likely that Jesus was a stranger to her and the townspeople. He did not ask if she had faith in him. The concern of Jesus throughout the story is mainly for the woman, not for her son. He simply had great sympathy for her. His own mother was a widow, and Jesus knew the problem which they had to face, especially those without sons. Jesus may have thought of his own mother's future plight. In this passage Luke used for the first time the title "Lord" for Jesus. In this context Jesus is depicted as the Lord over life and death. Although the title "Lord" is used frequently by Luke, Mark never used the title to refer to Jesus while he was on earth. See Luke 9:39; 12:42; 17:6; 19:8 as examples. "Jesus is Lord" became the first Christian creed in the early church.

Sympathy and compassion would not be enough to "command" someone to stop weeping as Jesus had done. He knew that he would aid this widow with more than words that day. Luke tells us that Jesus then moved over to the procession and "touched the bier." This time without a word he stopped the bearers. Although coffins were common in Egypt, they were not used in Palestine. A bier was made like a long wicker-work container to transport the body to the cemetery. Jesus was unconcerned with the ritual law which said he would be unclean if he touched the bier (Num. 19:11). To touch a corpse was even more defiling than to touch a leper. Jesus' concern was not for himself but for the widow. Imagine the sigh of surprise which must have arisen from the people as Jesus "touched the bier" to stop it.

Without any fanfare or notice Jesus issued a command: "Young man I say to you arise." Notice the emphatic "I say to you." His command is by his bare word alone. He himself wielded divine authority. You can only imagine what the bystanders must have wondered. His was a voice which cried-out to the dead. At the command of Jesus, the young man immediately "sat up and began to speak." "Sat up" is a rare Greek word which was used mostly by medical writers to describe a sick person sitting up in bed. Luke, the physician, used this verb only here and in Acts 9:40. It occurs no place else in the New Testament. The phrase "began to speak" was Luke's way of confirming the proof that the man was really alive. Following the restoration Jesus "gave him to his mother." Again, this suggests that the motive for this miracle was the compassion which Jesus had for the widow's loss. No one could have imagined that such an unexpected gift would come from a stranger on the road to the grave that afternoon. Now the widow could face the future with hope and security.

The response of the crowd was naturally fearful at first. They had never witnessed such supernatural powers before. Then their fear turned to praise as they thanked God for such power. The verb "has arisen" was the same one Jesus used to command the dead man to restoration. The crowd believed that Jesus was "a great prophet." His miracle may have reminded them of the Old Testament prophets, Elijah and Elisha, who had raised sons from the dead and restored them to their mothers. Read the accounts in I Kings 17:17-24; 2 Kings 4:21-37. This spectacular deed would be a sign that the messianic age was near.

A SHOCKING INTRUSION (7:36-39)

The other incident for our attention took place in the home of a Pharisee named Simon. The fact that Jesus ate in the homes of some of the Pharisees would seem to imply that he was not rejected by all of them. Luke recorded two other occasions when

Jesus dined with them. (See 11:37 and 14:1). Luke does not indicate Simon's motive for inviting Jesus for a meal. William Barclay has suggested three possibilities: (1) He might have been an admirer and sympathizer with Jesus. He showed him the respect of calling him rabbi and thought he might be a prophet. But his discourtesy of not providing Jesus a foot bath, the kiss, or perfume make this conclusion unlikely. (2) He may have used the occasion as a means of setting a trap to entice Jesus into saying something or doing something which might be used as a charge against him later. The respect he gave to Jesus, however, makes this appear improbable. (3) Maybe Simon was a man who simply liked to invite celebrities to his home. He saw this Galilean teacher as one he would examine with patronizing contempt. This might explain the mixture of respect and the omission of the basic Jewish courtesies.[17]

The phrase "sat at table" does not give a good picture of the setting. When a guest came to an eastern house for a meal, he left his sandals at the door. Instead of sitting, he would recline on a low couch with his feet behind him. Eastern hospitality required that the doors be left open at a banquet. Often beggars, curiosity seekers, those wanting to be entertained, admirers, or others would gather and stand around to see what was going on or if they might get some of the food. The woman was most likely in that crowd of spectators. Jesus, of course, was a guest.

The sinful woman was probably a prostitute. Since it appears obvious that she came prepared to anoint Jesus, she likely had already responded to his message of good news for the outcast and had found forgiveness. She had come up behind his couch to anoint him out of gratitude for her forgiveness. But before she could do this, she may have thought once again of her sinfulness and his forgiveness, and she began to weep. Not having a towel, and without thinking, she let down her hair and began to wipe Jesus' feet. Among the Jewish women disheveled hair was consid-

---

17 William Barclay, *The Gospel of Luke* (Philadelphia: The Westminster Press, 1956), 93-94.

ered shameful. The words "kissed his feet" indicate an action which was repeatedly done. She kept on kissing his feet fervently. To kiss the feet of Rabbis was a sign of reverence. Then she took the flask, commonly alabaster, from around her neck and anointed his feet.

The host, Simon, had been watching all that had happened between Jesus and this woman. Knowing what kind of a woman she was, Simon was offended by Jesus allowing the woman to touch him. Contemptuously he thought to himself, "if this man were a prophet, he would know that he has permitted himself to be made unclean by letting this woman touch him." Simon, therefore, concluded inwardly that Jesus could not be a true prophet. A man with true prophetic insight would have recognized her as a woman of the streets. It is unfortunate that tradition has identified this woman as Mary Magdalene. There is nothing to support that association in this passage, and there is no evidence to support the claim that Mary Magdalene was a prostitute. Others have even tried to identify the woman as Mary of Bethany. There is no support for this speculation.

JESUS PRONOUNCES FORGIVENESS (7:47-50)

In the background material (vv. 40-46), notice that Jesus called Simon by name indicating to him that he was aware of his thoughts. Then he told a brief parable about two people who had borrowed money and could not repay it. One owed the sum of five hundred denarii and the other fifty. The lender marked both accounts paid. Then Jesus asked: "Which of them will love him more?" Simon thought that the one was forgiven the greater debt would love him more. Jesus, then, revealed to Simon that be knew who this woman was. Simon had placed this woman in a category as a harlot and concluded that Jesus did not realize the woman's terrible reputation. Simon judged her only according to the slot he had placed her in. She was not a person to him but only a woman of ill fame, a harlot. She looked like all the rest of the streetwalkers to him. He could not see a face, a personality, a person.

Unlike Simon who had not shown Jesus the common courtesies due an honored guest, this woman had shown her great love by washing his feet with her tears, anointing them, and kissing them. Her unbounded gratitude and love were based on the forgiveness of her many sins. The New English Bible has given a good translation of verse 47: "And so, I tell you, her great love proves that her many sins have been forgiven; where little has been forgiven, little love is shown." This is a better translation than the KJV or the RSV since it notes clearly that she was not forgiven because of her great love. Her love was the evidence that she had already been forgiven. Her faith, not any works of love, had saved her (v. 50). Nevertheless, Jesus can say that she is forgiven because he sees the evidence of this forgiveness in her acts of love.

The words of Jesus, "Your sins are forgiven" (v. 48) are a confirmation of a sense of pardon she already had. The Greek words may be rendered "Your sins have been forgiven and remain forgiven." With these words Jesus offered her reassurance and made her forgiveness a public act. Those at the tables were disturbed by Jesus claiming that he could forgive sins (v. 49). The concept that only God could forgive sins was basic in Jewish theology. Many were probably shocked that any man would dare utter such words. But, as Luke was seeking to show, this One had the right to make divine claims because he was the Son of God. Turning to the woman, Jesus ignored his critics and said to her: "Your faith has saved you; go in peace." (v. 50) She had not necessarily been a worse sinner than Simon, but she had realized more deeply than he the awfulness of her sin, and, consequently she was overwhelmed at the greatness of her forgiveness. Her faith in Christ had enabled her to receive the grace of God's forgiveness. She could "go in peace" because she was at peace with herself and her God. She knew she was forgiven, so she could now live as a new woman- a woman with a future.

In the novel, *Brothers Karamazov*, Dostoevsky writes about a peasant woman who has fears about feeling forgiven by God. "There is no sin," the elder responds, "and there can be no sins on all the earth, which the Lord will not forgive to the truly repentant. Man cannot commit a sin so great as to exhaust the infinite love of God...Believe that God loves you as you cannot conceive, and that He loves you with your sin, in your sin." Quietly, he continues, "If I, a sinner, even as you are, am tender with you and have pity on you, how much more will God."[18]

The miracle of forgiveness is that a holy and righteous God extends his boundless love toward us while we are yet sinners and draws us to himself. Such everlasting love is beyond our understanding, but it is the biblical affirmation about the very nature of God. In his son, Jesus, we have seen this love demonstrated as he reached out to touch the untouchable and forgive the desperate and needy.

---

[18] Fyodor Dostoevsky, *The Brothers Karamazov* (Garden City, New York: International Collectors Library, n.d.),44-45.

God's Eternal Role of Redemption
Genesis, 12:1-3, Isaiah 45:22, 53:4-6; 56:1-8

The Church finds its purpose for existence as it realizes its redemptive mission in the world. The Church was not created to be served but was founded to be God's servant engaged in bringing about the salvation of men and women. Let us focus on "The World Mission of Our Church" by looking first at the biblical roots of the missionary teaching of the Old Testament.

The Role of Abraham

Our Scripture begins with the selection of Abraham as the human channel through whom God will establish a redemptive community. Genesis 12:3 should read "And by you all the families of the earth will bless themselves." This translation denotes that the followers of Abraham must have a similar faith to his if they are to be the recipients of divine blessings. God's redeeming grace will be mediated through human instrumentality. Originally the ancient Hebrews concept of redemption was a legal term.

It was used to describe the process by which persons or property could be reclaimed by the original owner upon payment of a designated amount of money. Since the basic idea involved in the Hebrew concept of redemption was the deliverance from a great loss or captivity, it became a vivid phrase later to describe God's saving grace.

God Within History

The God who is depicted in the Bible is not some remote deity "up there" apart from humanity and indifferent to him or her. The Scriptures bear witness to a God who is active within history. The deliverance from Egypt and other historical events were seen by Israel as signs of God's activity within history. Second Isaiah places the concept of redemption at the center of his teachings. Probably his highest concept is seen in the figure of the "Suffering Servant."

The Suffering Servant

Although scholars have interpreted the "Suffering Servant" in a variety of ways as the personification of the nation Israel, a remnant of Israel, a self-portrait of the prophet himself, or even another historical figure of the prophet's own age, the Christian Church has traditionally associated this figure with Jesus. No matter what was in the mind of the original writer, it seems clear that Jesus chose Isaiah's poetic description as the image of his own ministry. Isaiah points the way to a suffering redeemer, who will link his person and work together within history.

The prophet Isaiah was convinced that God would deliver his people from their captivity in Babylon. This deliverance would be for all who remained faithful to God. Although the main emphasis of Isaiah was upon national freedom from bondage, a wider truth of God's universal redemption seems evident. "My house shall be called a house of prayer for all peoples." The eternal purpose of God's redemption has included all persons of all races. We cannot exclude those whom God has redeemed.

The Recklessness of Idolatry

Isaiah 44:6-20

A small boy turns to his mother at the dinner table and asks: "Who made God?" "No one" is the response usually given. God has always existed. Nevertheless, men and women seem to be continuously making God in his or her own image or in the form of something with which one is familiar. In the "do-it-yourself" craze of our day, we seek to be self-sufficient. We want to be able to do our own repairs and odd jobs. This tendency has been carried over into our religion. We seem to want a "do-it-yourself" religion, in which we maintain, direct, and control our own life. Isaiah saw this same sort of "home-made" religion and the folly that resulted from it in his own day.

The Ridiculousness of Idolatry

Writing with a biting and ridiculing pen, Isaiah formulates a satire that denounces the absurdity of idolatry. In vivid detail he notes how a blacksmith shapes an idol in his forge and beats it into the desired shape. The carpenter craftsman also carefully designs the image he wants. Isaiah observes that the craftsman is extremely diligent in his selection of the proper tree in the forest. He then cuts it down and utilizes the same log to build a fire to warm himself, and to cook his dinner. From the part of the wood that is left over, he makes a god. He then falls before this god made from leftover firewood and worships it. He bows before the wooden object his own hands have made and pleads with it to deliver him. Isaiah argues that this is irrational. The creator seeks salvation from its own creation. The prophet is searing in his ridicule and scorn of this comical, homemade god.

The Futility of Idolatry

The negative emphases of Isaiah's satire was designed to warn Israel of the futility of idol worship. They were now captives in Babylon, but the prophet was not convinced that this meant that the war gods of their conquerors were more powerful than Jehovah. Behind the ironical words of Isaiah was the truth that there is but one God, who alone is sovereign over all the earth. His satire is a plea to his own people to remain firm in their monotheism.

Today we are too sophisticated to fall down in worship before a stone or wooden image, but our religious interests are often reserved only for the leftovers of our efforts, time, and money. Our modern idolatry centers around financial security, prestige, popularity, external comfort, and happiness. Whatever assumes first place of importance in our lives, this has become our god. This choice proves to be a bad bargain if it is less than the eternal God of the universe. Redemption originates with God's initiative, and we are not able to control or create it. We respond to God's revelation and in this encounter, we know what God is like. God refuses to be made according to our specifications but demands that we meet the Eternal God according to the divine dimension.

Sharing Christ's Name to the World

Matthew 1:21; Mark 10:42-45; Luke 19:1-10

"What's in a name?" we often ask with Shakespeare's Romeo. Nevertheless, we are keenly aware of the images some names bring to our minds. What flashes into our memory when we read the names of Moses, David, Isaiah, Paul, Peter, Luther, Schweitzer, Nero, Genghis Khan, Hitler, Stalin, Castro, or Putin? Today a person's name stands for little more than an identification tag, or the way one individual is distinguished from another. Parents sometimes select a name for a newborn child because of its association with a relative or a friend, or simply because they like the name. Among the ancient Israelites a person's name was chosen for a higher function than simple recognition or a pleasing "ring." The Hebrew people believed that a person's name contained something of the life and power of the bearer himself or herself. They considered a person's name to be an expression of one's essential personality and character. In the Old Testament to know God's name meant to know the God who had revealed God's nature and character through divine redemptive activity within history.

The Name Jesus

The New Testament declares that God has revealed God's self uniquely through Jesus Christ. Those who believe in his "name" can become children of God. (John 1:12) In the announcement of the birth of Christ. it was declared that he would be named Jesus.

The name Jesus itself means "the salvation of the Lord," but his mission is emphasized further with the phrase "for he shall save his people from their sins!" (Matt. 1:21) At his birth itself, the gospel writers affirm that the mission of Jesus in the world was to be concerned with redemption.

Throughout the gospels the name Jesus is used of our Lord more than six hundred times. His name was in essence a one-word summary of his mission. Paul proclaims that the gospel of Jesus Christ is the "power of God unto salvation to everyone who believes." (Rom. 1:16) Jesus himself declared that "the Son of man came to seek and to save the lost." (Luke 19:10) The parables of the lost sheep, lost coin and prodigal son also present the mission of Jesus as a redemptive one. When Jesus began his ministry, he chose the words from Isaiah's image of the Suffering Servant as the picture of his liberating mission: "He has sent me to proclaim release to the Captives... to set at liberty those who are oppressed." (Luke 4:18)

THE CALL TO SERVICE

In sharp contrast to the desires of James and John who wanted positions of political prestige in the kingdom of Christ, Jesus declares that greatness is not to be measured in terms of the amount of power one person has over others but is determined in terms of service. If anyone wishes to be great, he or she must become a servant (in the Greek, slave). Here Jesus attempts to drive home the point that the Christian life is centered around giving of self not in self-seeking. He points to his own life as an example. He came not "to be served but to serve." The ultimate expression of his concept of service and love is stated in his willingness to make the supreme sacrifice of his own life for others. Many pictures may flash into our minds when Jesus speaks of his willingness to give his life as "a ransom for many." No matter what else may be implied in the statement, it is, at least, a depiction of the costly nature of salvation. God's grace is not cheap. The cross marks within history the cost to God for our redemption.

The Example of Zacchaeus

The story of Zacchaeus is one story among many within the New Testament in which Jesus is pictured as a seeker of those who are "lost." Jesus sought out Zacchaeus to restore the misused and unused potential within him. Barriers of social, economic, or racial distinctions did not stand in the way of Jesus when a person was in need. Although Zacchaeus had become wealthy as a contractor-in-chief of local taxes, Jesus realized he still was in "want." Zacchaeus was "up a tree" because of his moral and ethical failure, but only when he found that Jesus would accept him and would voluntarily identify with a man of a despised profession, did Zacchaeus respond to his invitation to discipleship. As a sign of the inward change in his life, Zacchaeus decided to make a fourfold restitution for any frauds he had committed, and also to give half of his possessions to the poor. This was far more than the Jewish law required. Zacchaeus was aware, however. that words were not enough to indicate a changed life but one's actions also had to demonstrate the price of a life committed to Jesus Christ. The experience of Zacchaeus was an example of one person's response to the One who had come "to seek and to save that which was lost."

Christ's Commission to the Individual Christian

Luke 10:1-2; John 17:18-23; Matthew 28:16-20

Plant life may be able to bear its seeds and multiply spontaneously, but the continuance of the Christian church is contingent upon the deliberate action of its believers. Each believer is responsible for sharing the "good news" with others. If the Church loses sight of its missionary responsibility, it forfeits its reason for being. The purpose of the Church is not to become an exclusive club, content only with its own welfare and perpetuation and concerned only with paraphernalia and trivial causes. The Church was created with no small task in mind; its purpose is to be the redemptive force in the world.

Substitutes for Service

During the Civil War one could pay another person to fight for him and remain uninvolved in the conflict. Sometimes it would appear that we have revived this practice within our churches, if not elsewhere. Often, we attempt to "hire" someone else to serve and witness for us. The pastors of our churches are often considered as the congregation's substitute who plays the religious game for others. The pastor is similar to a playing coach. He is coaching the team, seeking to give them guidance and direction, and while he or she is also actively involved within the game, that minister does not and cannot do all the work. Within the church, the pastor seeks to serve, lead, and work, but the whole congregation has been commissioned to serve without reservation as ministers. If the church is to recover its sense of mission in the world, it must rediscover its vocation of witness. The lay ministry must accept its share in the ministry of proclaiming the gospel at home and abroad. Disciples must become apostles.

All Followers Are Ministers

The lesson from this passage clearly demonstrates that Jesus did not have a "hireling clergy" in mind for his ambassadors. All of his disciples were "lay" ministers. Within Luke's universal view of the gospel, his reference to the seventy which Jesus sent out on their mission two by two could be an allusion to the seventy elders of Moses (Num. 11:16-24) or to the number of the Sanhedrin, the supreme council of the Jews. Along with the disciples who had already been sent earlier into northern Palestine (Luke 9:1-6), the seventy were appointed (set apart) to go into southern Galilee.

Sharing the Good News

SET APART FOR SERVICE

The high priestly prayer of Jesus, as recorded in the seventeenth chapter of John reveals Christ's version of the mission, consecration, glory, and unity of his disciples. Jesus did not pray that his disciples might find escape from the world, but he sent them, as he had been sent by God, into the world to lead men and women to God. Jesus prayed that his disciples might be consecrated by the truth. The word consecrate comes from the Greek word, *hagios,* which means "different" or "separate." The disciples of Christ are those who have been set apart for a special task. Their character and lives are to be that different ingredient in the world that can help bring about transformation.

THE MISSION IMPERATIVE

The final words of Jesus as recorded in Matthew 28:19-20, symbolize the charter of Christian missions. Although the commission is directed to the disciples of Jesus, this does not exclude the contemporary Christian. The word disciple means learner, one who is seeking to learn from the Master teacher. All Christians should be learners, continuing to grow in the Christian faith. The final words of Jesus, then, are directed to every disciple. In the Greek there is only one imperative given in the "great commission" and that is the one translated "teach" or better rendered "disciple" or "make disciples." "Go ye" is not an imperative but a participle and should read "going". Going (or as you go) disciple all the nations, baptizing them...teaching them...Jesus assumed that his followers would be going, and as they went, their purpose was to make disciples of all nations.

THE CONTEMPORARY CHALLENGE OF MISSIONS

The lack of genuine Christian commitment on the part of many church members is one of the most serious problems confronting the Church today. Just as a person was bound by a cord of faithfulness to God in the Old Testament understanding of the covenant, he or she is now bound by a commitment of faith to Jesus Christ in the New Covenant. The Christian today needs to affirm: "For I am proud of the gospel: it is God's saving power for everyone who has faith" (Rom. 1:16, Moffatt). God has imparted to the Christian a great trust. God has given to us the gospel to share with the world, a gospel of good news of redeeming grace for all persons. Fidelity is essential on the part of the believer if the good news is to be shared. Someone has said that Christianity is always just one generation away from extinction. It is the responsibility of this present generation to bear witness to Christ. How can anyone keep to oneself what is the greatest force, power, and redemption in the world? There is no place for neutrality as a Christian witness. Not to share with another the grace one has received in Christ is equivalent to extinguishing it.

Paul's Method of Witnessing
1 Corinthians 1:17-18; 2:1-8

When the Apostle Paul wrote to the Corinthian church, he was not new to the work of Christian missions. Fifteen years of labor, hope, love, sorrow, and suffering had passed since he first responded to the call on the road to Damascus. Except for the city of Ephesus. Paul had worked longer in Corinth to establish a church than in any other city. Several years later, while he was in Ephesus, Paul learned of the problems in the Corinthian Church and wrote to them, hoping to give them some guidance and instruction regarding their divisions and misunderstandings. In this correspondence we get some insight into the Pauline approach to Christian witnessing.

Factions in the Early Church

The first four chapters of the first Corinthian letter are concerned with the problem of the sectarian divisions in the church. Factions had arisen within the church and had divided the congregation into sects which identified themselves with particular leaders and teachers, such as Paul, Apollos, Cephas, and others. Paul attempted to stress in this letter that he wanted the church united in Christ and that he was not seeking Paulinism converts. The reference to the fact that he had personally baptized only a few, Stephanos, Crispus, and Gaius, (1:14) did not mean that Paul was trying to minimize baptism. He simply was trying to get his converts to identify with Christ and not himself. Baptism, in Paul's mind, was subordinated to the proclamation of the gospel.

Baptism was a function that could be performed by another, Paul indicated, and was not the true apostolic work. This primary task was to preach the power of the cross of Christ.

God's Redeeming Grace

The message of the cross is not just the story about the crucifixion of Jesus but the good news that "God was in Christ reconciling the world to himself." It is the message of God's redeeming grace. To the cultured Greek mind "the preaching of the cross" sounded like foolishness. From the root of the Greek word for foolishness, we get the English word "moron". This word reveals something of the disdain and ridicule the Greeks directed against Paul's preaching. The phrase "to them that perish" is literally "those who are on the way to destruction," or "those destroying themselves."

The Cross as the Power of God

To those who have felt the redeeming grace of God, the cross is the power of God. Paul states that those who reject the gospel and those who receive it are in the course of perishing and being saved respectively. The New Testament view of salvation is concerned with the past, present, and future (Rom. 8:24; 10:9; Eph. 2:5·; 1 Cor. 15:2). In the cross of Jesus Christ, God has exerted the greatest expression of the power of his sacrificial love, and, as men and women respond to this love, they experience the power of God's redemption. The central theme of Paul's preaching is the cross of Christ.

Paul Did Not Use Rhetoric to Proclaim the Gospel

Unlike many itinerant Greek teachers of wisdom, who emphasized rhetoric and pretentious eloquence, Paul declared that he proclaimed an unadorned gospel, in order that men and women might respond to the power of God and not be swayed by his oratorical ability. Paul had discarded the eloquence of words, so that faith might not be grounded in clever reasoning and be merely an intellectual response to the gospel. He was keenly aware that it often is easier to change men and women's minds than their lives. The first two verses of Chapter two reveal the manner Paul did not use in his preaching at Corinth, while verses three through five indicate his actual method. He came weak, timid, and trembling. aware of his own limitations. He came without the desire to entice men and women by his own wisdom and eloquence.

THE MYSTERY OF GOD'S REDEMPTION

The wisdom of God, which Paul proclaimed, could not be reduced to an intellectual response to a set of propositions or a system of beliefs. "The wisdom of God is a mystery" of which Paul speaks, is the wisdom which was personally revealed through God's activity in his Son within history. The word "mystery" is one of Paul's significant terms, and he returns to it frequently In his writings. "Mystery" is not a reference here to something that remains unknown or a puzzle but refers to that which was previously unknown but now is openly known. The reference is to the redemptive work of God through Christ.

THE INCARNATION OF CHRIST

The apostle Paul's message was concerned with "the Word made flesh." Far from being an abstract or impersonal term, the Word describes the personal incarnation of God within history in Jesus Christ. Knowledge about a person is not the same as knowing him personally. Someone may say that he knows something "about" God, but this is not the same as declaring that he or she knows God "personally." Paul's approach to witnessing was to lead people to a commitment to the One who was the living Word and not to convince them about some words or ideas about him. He did not want men or women to settle for ideas about God, when personal communion with God was available through Jesus Christ.

Paul's Plan for Expansion

Acts 13:2-3, 46-48; Romans 15:18-24

If someone had attempted to convince the leaders of the Roman Empire that the influence from Jesus Christ and his small band of followers would soon spread across the empire and eventually be carried around the world, they would probably have found the statement amusing and ridiculous. But the unbelievable thing is that the disciples of Christ actually did accomplish what appeared to be an "impossible mission."

The Early Expansion of Christianity

Before the first century drew to a close, and without any of the modern means of travel or communication, the Christian gospel was carried over three thousand miles from Jerusalem. The way the early church was able to expand its work so rapidly was due primarily to the efforts of the Apostle Paul. Our attention here focuses on Paul's method of spreading the gospel to all persons.

The Antioch Church

The church at Antioch was one of the outstanding New Testament Churches. The followers of Jesus were first called Christians at Antioch. (Acts 11:26} It was the church at Antioch that sent Paul and Barnabas with an offering to the distressed churches of Judea. This church also led in breaking down the racial barriers which had separated the Jews and Gentiles. The Scripture in Acts describes the role the church at Antioch played in sending out the first "foreign" missionaries.

The worshipers in the church at Antioch felt the leadership of the Spirit of God to begin the difficult task of sharing the gospel where it had not been heard before. The leaders in the church were a mixed group from various backgrounds. Simeon, who was also called Niger (meaning black). may have been from Africa. Some scholars have even speculated that this man may have been the same Simon of Cyrene (in North Africa) who carried the cross of Jesus. (Luke 23:26) The church responded to the guidance of God's spirit and released for missionary service Paul and Barnabas, two of their most outstanding and able leaders. It might be of interest to note that the same verb is used in Greek for "separate me" in this passage that Paul used to describe his call in Romans 1:1 and Galatians 1:15. This missionary endeavor came as a divine directive to Paul and Barnabas to carry the gospel further.

Sharing the Gospel with Gentiles

Paul's chief approach in preaching the gospel had been to speak first in the Jewish synagogue. At a Sabbath day's service in the synagogue at Antioch of Pisidia, Paul encountered violent and outspoken opposition from the Jews to his message. Gentiles had crowded into the synagogue to hear Paul, but instead of rejoicing at the response, the Jewish people were enraged and aroused against Paul and Barnabas, because the Jews realized that the Gentiles were by-passing Judaism for Christ. This self-exclusive attitude of the Jews at Antioch forced the dramatic decision in which Paul turned to the Gentiles with the gospel. Paul had not excluded the Jews. He had come to them first with the message, but their rigid Jewish nationalism and narrow provincialism had caused them to exclude themselves. Verse 46 is literally translated: "Since you thrust it (the word of God) from you, and judge yourselves unworthy of eternal life, behold, we turn to the Gentiles."

A Wider Vision of the Gospel

The violent action and words of the Jews provoked the momentous decision of Paul and Barnabas. Now they turned away from directing their mission directly to the Jewish synagogue and began a worldwide ministry. This decision met with great rejoicing among the Gentiles and made it easier to reach them, but it created greater hostility among the Jews and made it more difficult to witness to them. Although Jewish persecution forced Paul and Barnabas to leave Antioch, they left with a wider vision of the universal gospel and left behind in Antioch a church which was a part of God's "new covenant."

Paul's Vision to Carry the Gospel Further

In the last few verses of his letter to the church at Rome, Paul speaks on a personal note, indicating his understanding of his mission as an apostle to the Gentiles. He considered his major responsibility to be a pioneer missionary, one who did the groundwork that others might build on it. He states that he has "fully preached the gospel of Christ." This does not mean that Paul had evangelized the whole world personally, but presumably denoted that he had proclaimed a gospel which was sufficient to establish churches wherever he had preached. He had preached to those who had never heard the gospel and had founded new churches. He left the responsibility of developing these churches largely to others. Paul is writing to the Roman Church from Corinth and indicates that he hopes to travel from there to Jerusalem, then to Rome and finally to Spain. Spain was at the far distant, western end of the Roman Empire and was considered the limit of known civilization in Paul's day. Even in his travel plans, Paul indicates the vast horizon which he saw unfolding for his mission outreach. The gospel was for the whole world.

Undergirding Missions with Prayer & Giving
Matthew 9:35-38; Romans 15:30-33; 1 Timothy 2:1-15

Anyone who studies carefully the life of Christ, as presented in the gospels, is aware of the numerous occasions in which Jesus engaged in prayer. Christ constantly spoke about the power and importance of prayer. But Christ did more than merely talk about the significance of prayer. His whole life was one of open, continuous communion with his Father, and he was eager that his followers might find and share in this powerful communion. We were created for fellowship with God and outside this relationship, we find life empty and meaningless. Jesus revealed in his life the powerful role that prayer plays in opening the avenue of communion with God's spirit.

The Compassion of Jesus

Jesus did not envision prayer as autosuggestion but saw it as an effective means of directing one's relationship to God and his or her fellow man or woman. The verses from Matthew's Gospel describe the evangelistic and mission trip which Jesus made through all the towns and villages of Galilee. His ministry was depicted as a threefold undertaking of preaching, teaching, and healing. The crowds that came to Jesus moved him deeply and he saw them as sheep without a shepherd. The Greek word used to describe the compassion which Jesus felt for the people is the strongest word in Greek for pity and depicts one who has been moved to the utter depths of his being. The people "fainted and were scattered abroad" is a descriptive verse of the sad and impoverished spiritual condition of the people. The spiritual leaders had harassed and bewildered them and had placed endless burdens upon them instead of giving them guidance and strength. Jesus was keenly aware that the people were ready for the good news." The harvest field was ripe and ready for reapers. Jesus also knew that this task would require many workers, and he instructs his disciples to pray that God will "send forth", literally "to push out or to drive out," laborers for this task. Prayer was essential if the need for workers was to be met.

Paul's Request for Prayer

Paul appeals to the Church at Rome for their prayers concerning the journey he has to make to Judea. Paul had hoped that he would be able to travel to Rome and then on to Spain, but he first had to deliver the offering to the church in Jerusalem, which he had spent two years collecting in small weekly sums (I Cor. 16:2). This offering was to be used by the needy Christians in Jerusalem. It was Paul's hope that this love offering from the Gentile churches might serve as a means of uniting the Jewish and Gentile Christians. Paul's request for prayer was concerned with two items. First, he was aware of the personal danger to his own life from the unbelieving Jews and secondly, he was hopeful that the love offering might serve as a peace offering to the Jewish Christians in Jerusalem. On other occasions, Paul had mentioned the bitter prejudices which many of the Jerusalem Christians had retained regarding the Gentiles. If these prayers were answered, Paul then planned to travel to his Roman friends and share in the joy and rest of their fellowship.

Paul's Answered Prayer

The Apostle Paul himself is a clear example that God does not always answer our prayers as we expect. (See Acts 21) The non-Christian Jews in Jerusalem accused Paul of defiling the temple by bringing Gentiles into it, and they would have killed him if the Roman soldiers had not rescued him. Paul was arrested and then sent to Rome as a prisoner. His prayer was answered but not in the manner he had expected. He still came to Rome, however, and, while a prisoner, he wrote letters to encourage struggling Christian churches. Through these letters, Paul's influence has reached further than he could have ever anticipated.

The Universal Nature of Prayer

The passage from Timothy is concerned with the scope of prayer in public worship. Although it is possible to show distinctions between the nearly synonymous terms of "supplications, prayers, intercessions, and thanksgivings," the major emphasis is not with the shades of difference in these various forms of prayer but is concerned with the universal nature of prayer. Prayer is urged here primarily for others and is to be made for all persons regardless of class or condition. One class in particular is singled out, the king and others in authority, who, at various times, persecuted the Christians. Here the universal nature of the gospel is revealed. Christians are urged to pray even for those who are persecuting them. This reveals the sympathy and extent of the Christian outreach. God's love extends to all men and women. Christians are urged to pray for all persons because God is seeking to bring salvation to all men and women. We link our lives with God's eternal longing for human redemption, when we engage in prayerful concern for others.

Giving: Essential for Missions

Romans 15:25-27; 2 Corinthians 9:6-15

One of the Apostle Paul's greatest desires was to travel to Rome with the gospel and then journey on to Spain. Before he could take this journey, however. he believed it essential to travel in the opposite direction, east, to Jerusalem. Although Paul was aware of the dangers and difficulties which might confront him in Jerusalem, he believed that he needed to deliver personally an offering which he had collected from the Gentile Christians for the poor Christians in Jerusalem. Several years had been spent by the apostle in collecting this offering, and it had been raised in small weekly sums as he traveled from church to church.

The Christians as Saints

The word "saints," as used in this Roman passage and in other places in the New Testament, does not refer to a select group of pious Christians but is a reference for everyone in the early church who was a Christian. The word "Christian" occurs only three times in the New Testament. But in fifteen of the twenty-seven New Testament writings, the followers of Christ in the early churches are called saints. Christians are saints because they are "in Christ" and have been "set apart" by the "Holy One of God."

The Offering for the Jerusalem Church

The contribution, which the churches in Macedonia and Achaia had raised, was a free and voluntary act on their part. But these churches were aware of their spiritual indebtedness to the mother church in Jerusalem. The first church in Jerusalem had shared its "spiritual things," or better translated "spiritual blessings." with the Greek Gentiles in Macedonia and Achaia. The Israel of God was no longer limited to the Jews but, through Christ, a "new Israel" and a "new covenant" had been formed which also included the Gentiles. Now the Greek Christians could assist their needy Christian brothers in the mother church. The book of Acts records the method the church at Jerusalem had used in "sharing everything in common" to meet the needs of its members (Acts 4:32-34). But twenty years later famine and persecution had left the Jerusalem Church in a weak condition. Paul hoped that this love offering would not only meet the physical needs of the Jerusalem Church but serve as a factor in uniting the Jewish and Gentile Christians.

Paul as a Fund Raiser

In the eighth and ninth chapters of 2 Corinthians, Paul discussed the part which the Church at Corinth was to take in the special love offering he was collecting for the church at Jerusalem. These chapters contain in a brief form Paul's philosophy of Christian stewardship. Titus had been put in charge of this offering, and Paul was urging the church to get busy in collecting it, because he would be coming by soon to collect it and carry it on to Jerusalem. This passage reveals the "down to earth" nature of the Apostle Paul. Although he was a great preacher, theologian, mission organizer, and leader, he was still aware of the practical necessity of financial support if churches are to survive and grow. The great apostle could even be a "fund-raiser" when the need demanded it.

Giving as a Sign of Christian Love

Paul did not consider it below his calling to be concerned with small and practical matters as well as deep, theological concerns. He was aware that spiritual and material concerns are bound closely together. Paul compares Christian giving to the sowing of seeds. If a man sows seeds meagerly, he cannot expect a large crop in return, but if he sows with plenty of seeds, he will receive a large crop. Some might state that the reward motive here is a low appeal. The New Testament does not avoid this appeal, but the emphasis is on spiritual rewards and not material blessings. This passage also stresses that giving is not to be based on one's impulse of the moment; nor should it be done because one feels he or she cannot avoid it and is compelled to contribute. The Christian has learned that a selfish person is never rich. The Christian should give cheerfully in recognition of God's gracious love to him. Paul believed that this love offering would be a visible sign of the church's praise for God's gift, and a generous spirit would also reveal to the church at Jerusalem that high quality of the Gentile Christians. The offering, Paul envisioned, would also draw the Christian churches into a greater unity of fellowship and concern.

God's Unspeakable Gift

In concluding this section Paul expresses his thanks for "God's unspeakable gift," namely Jesus Christ. The unspeakable nature is the recognition of God's gracious self-giving to humanity. Here Paul unveils the real foundation of all genuine Christian giving. The Christian motive for giving is an inner commitment to the Christ-like way, which is paradoxically that we save only by spending ourselves; receive only in giving and find only by losing (Luke 9:24).

Witnessing: The Way of Missions Under the Guidance of the Holy Spirit
2 Corinthians 4:5-18

Nearly everyone is familiar with the function and purpose of a witness in a courtroom. A witness is asked to relate what he or she has seen or heard personally. Hearsay, opinions, or interpretations are not allowed as a valid function of a witness. A person testifies only to what one has witnessed personally. Jesus said of his followers, "You shall be my witnesses" (Acts 1:8). The writer of the small first epistle of John speaks of the personal nature of the Christian witness. "That which was from the beginning, which we have heard, which we have seen with our eyes, which we have looked upon and touched with our hands, concerning the word of life…that which we have seen and heard we proclaim also to you" (I John l: 1, 3). The words, "heard," "seen" and "touched" are personal words which indicate the personal nature of his witness.

The Great Commission

The final words of Jesus, as recorded in Matthew 28:19-20, and often called the "great commission," contain only one imperative, "make disciples." The words translated "Go you, baptize and teach" are not imperatives but participles. "Going (or as you go) disciple all the nations, baptizing them…teaching them." Jesus believed that his disciples would be going to witness to his redeeming grace.

Paul's Real Motive for Preaching

In 2 Corinthians 4:5-18, we are able to sense something of the internal and external struggle in which the Apostle Paul engaged as he proclaimed the "good news" of Christ. Paul was aware that some had accused him of having improper motives, and he wanted to set the record straight. He stated that his chief aim had been to preach Christ, and he had not attempted to display his own cleverness. Paul pointed to his own conversion experience as evidence that he had experienced in his own life the same creative power that had created the world. Paul had confronted God's creative activity within the face (presence) of Jesus Christ.

Paul was aware that the "knowledge of God's glory in the face of Jesus Christ," (the revelator, of what God was like, the gospel), was a priceless treasure contained in a frail, clay vessel. Here Paul frankly acknowledges his physical and spiritual weaknesses. The earthenware jar is symbolic of Paul's realization of his own weakness and his absolute dependence upon God. He describes his infirmities in several paradoxical statements.

Service Involves Sacrifice

Frustrations and pressures weighed down upon him but did not defeat him; he was confused but never without hope, persecuted but assured of God's loyal presence; and was knocked down but not ultimately defeated. Paul indicates that he is able to endure his own suffering as he realizes the cost of discipleship. He was aware that there is "no crown without a cross." Verses 10-11 indicate that Paul had united his life with Christ and was willing to share in the suffering and hardships which it entailed. Paul knew that the servant might have to suffer the same sort of pain, shame and suffering which Jesus endured at the end of his life. But he was also convinced that Jesus suffered in and through those who have committed themselves to his service.

THE ASSURANCE OF RESURRECTION

The Apostle Paul affirmed his belief that if he shared in sacrificial suffering, he would also share in the resurrection of Christ. He was willing to suffer and die, because he firmly believed he could draw upon the same power that raised up Christ from the dead to raise him from the grave to dwell with the living Lord. Paul stated a similar position in Romans 8:18 when he said: "I consider that the sufferings of this present time are not worth comparing with the glory that is to be revealed to us."

PAUL'S VOCATION AS A WITNESS

Paul had endured suffering for the sake of the church, in the conviction that others would be led to Christ through his sacrificial witness and be able to share in the eternal life he had found in Christ. The personal encounter which Paul had with Jesus Christ on the Damascus Road and the continuing vital relationship with him are paramount to Paul's understanding of his "vocation of witness." He knew that his redemptive experience with Christ was personal. but that it could never be private. He was compelled from within, and overjoyed at the privilege, to share with others the love of God which he knew. In another letter to one of the early churches, Paul states his view of Christian witness. "I appeal to you therefore, brethren, by the mercies of God, to present your bodies as a living sacrifice, holy and acceptable to God, which is your spiritual worship" (Rom. 12:1).

WORSHIP AND SERVICE MUST BE UNITED

The sacrificial words and deeds of the Christian are the outward expression of one's worship of God. Worship and service are bound together; our worship needs to materialize into service, and our service reflects the depth of our worship.

THE HOLY SPIRIT: GUIDING MISSIONS

John 16:7-14; Acts 1:4-8 5:29-32

How many times have we said, "If only I could have seen Jesus in the flesh and have heard his voice, what a difference it would have made in my faith." But in the Fourth Gospel, Jesus tells his disciples that the opposite will be true. "It is expedient for you that I go away." The Greek word for "expedient" means profitable or advantageous. The bewildered disciples must have wondered how it could be to their advantage to lose their Master. Jesus states that it is essential that he depart his bodily presence if the Holy Spirit, Greek "Paracletes", is to come. The word "*paracletos*" is usually translated "Helper" or "Comforter," but sometimes it has been rendered as "advocate," in the sense of one who stands by an accused person in court to defend and support him or her. While Jesus was in the flesh, he was limited by time and place. His physical withdrawal allowed his spirit to be free and available for all people everywhere.

THE HOLY SPIRIT

The words Holy Spirit. and especially "Holy Ghost", are confusing and difficult terms for the modern mind to grasp. The word "ghost" conveys pictures of an apparition today. and the word "spirit" carries somewhat of the same vague connotation. In the seventeenth century, when the King James Version of the Bible was written, the word ghost meant a personal entity or life. Today when we say that someone, or something has spirit, we mean it has life and vitality. The phrase Holy Spirit refers to the living activity of God's presence in the world. In the passage from John's Gospel, two aspects of the work of the Spirit are summarized.

THE WORK OF THE HOLY SPIRIT

First, the Spirit will reprove, convince, or convict an unbelieving world for rejecting Christ. He will do this in three ways:

First, the Spirit will convict humanity of the sin of not believing in Christ. Unbelief is of course, a sin, but the significant truth here is the realization that the rejection of Christ is evidence of man and woman's sin. Second, the Holy Spirit will convince men and women of the righteousness of Christ. When Christ was tried and crucified, He was regarded as a criminal and a heretic. But the resurrection and the triumphant exaltation of Jesus to the Father vindicated the claims Jesus had made. Third, the Spirit will convince men and women of God's judgment against the power of evil. The death of Christ will not be regarded as a defeat, but the Spirit will demonstrate the power and victory of the cross and the risen Lord over the forces of evil. Defeat will be turned into victory.

THE SPIRIT'S ACTIVITY

A second aspect of the Spirit's activity is described in verses 12-14. Jesus indicate that his work was limited by the shortness of his time with the disciples and by their capacity to understand and grasp the truth at their present spiritual maturity. He had started them on their spiritual pilgrimage, but the Holy Spirit would come after Christ's departure and lead them into a deeper understanding of his life and ministry. One of the significant insights disclosed within this passage is the continuous activity of God's spirit. God has uniquely revealed himself through his Son, and the Scriptures bear witness to the Son. but he is not just a person who lived in the past and was written about in a book. He is the living Lord, who seeks to reveal himself to humanity in the present.

THE BAPTISM OF THE HOLY SPIRIT

The Book of Acts discloses that Jesus had instructed his disciples not to leave Jerusalem until they had received the power of the Holy Spirit. Jesus gently corrects his disciples when they asked him if it was time to set up a political kingdom. He challenges them with a universal mission which sets no political limits. God's Kingdom could not be determined by a calendar but would be established through the witnessing of the disciples of Christ. The "baptism of the Holy Spirit" is the empowering of the disciples by the living presence of Christ. who had promised his disciples that "I am with you always, to the close of the age" (Matt. 28:20). The disciples are not to wait for the world to come to Jerusalem, but they will begin there and move into Judea, and then reach out to the Simi Jewish region of Samaria and finally witness to the whole world.

The Outreach of the Church

The emphasis here is not merely on geographical expansion, but the necessity of overcoming national and racial boundaries as well. The Church began with a mission task as its basic function and continues to exist as the "true Church" only as it seeks to realize its origin and purpose for existence. The outreach of the Church is never simply concerned with what man or woman is able to accomplish but is an affirmation of what their spirit is able to execute when empowered by the Divine Spirit. In Jesus Christ, we experience authentic joy which enables us to live the authentic joyful life. And we want to share that meaningful experience with others.[19]

---

19   C. S. Lewis, *Surprised by Joy* (New York: Harcourt, Brace and Co., 1955), 233-234.

Reasons for Attending Church
Hebrews 12:22-25

There are many reasons people don't go to church. In an article published in *The Christian Century*, "I don't go to church," Adam J. Copeland, a professor at Luther Seminary in St. Paul, Minnesota, list reasons why he and his wife have stopped attending church. He acknowledges that they don't need a church to be perfect, but just to be "enough" community, worship, and seeking of truth. "I still have hope in the power of the Christian community," Copeland concludes, "even after all the difficult church visits."[20]

I have not given up on the church and, therefore, I want to put the primary focus on why we should go to church. Let us turn now to these reasons. I know some people who go to church because it is simply part of their family heritage. They go today because their parents brought them when they were young. Others go because their friends are there, or because the church is friendly, or it has good programs for children, youth, or adults. Others like the preacher or the music. These reasons for going to church are not wrong. We all want a church that offers a variety of programs and meets needs in our life, but our reasons for going to church should be much deeper and on a more profound level than

---

[20] Adam J. Copeland, "Why I don't go to church," The Christian Century (March 27, 2019), 11.

these kinds of surface reasons that we often select. I offer to you the following suggestions.

Provides an Oasis Where We Can Worship God

First, we should go to church because it is the place that is set aside to worship God. It is the place built where we can gather together as a community of faith and declare as Isaiah did: "Holy, holy, holy is the Lord God of hosts." The church you worship in and other churches are built to acknowledge the reality of the living God who is beyond us. We say with the Westminster Confession that "the chief end of man is to glorify God and to enjoy him forever." We come to church to glorify him and to attest to his reality. The word worship means "worth ship." We worship because we ascribe great worth to God. He is the One worthy of our worship. We come to adore him, pray to him, and to kneel in thanksgiving before his awesome presence. His higher worth forces us to get our priorities in order. Worship acknowledges that the material world is not all there is to reality. The spiritual world is real, and we bow before the Creator of all of life.

We gather together in worship acknowledging that there is a need beyond ourselves which we cannot satisfy in and of ourselves. The need for spiritual help beyond ourselves is reflected all through our society today even by those who claim to be non-religious. Why do so many people read horoscopes? Why do people buy Ouija boards? Why is there so much interest in Eastern religions, especially Zen Buddhism? Why is there so much interest in spiritualism? All this interest attests to the fact that there is an awareness on the part of many that there is a spiritual force beyond themselves which they long to know. We gather in worship to acknowledge the reality of that God.

You may have walked through your yard or by a house that has been abandoned and come across a board lying in the grass. When you kicked the board over, did you notice what the vegetation underneath that board looked like when the board had been lying there for a long time? The vegetation under the board had turned white and become distorted. If the board is there long enough, it will kill the vegetation. Why does the vegetation look like that? It has been cut off from the sunlight - its source of life. Our lives, when they are cut off from worship, become distorted and lose their true color. We lose contact with the source for high standards and values. We become empty and distorted, because we are cut off from the very source of our being itself - God.

Worship is not to be a momentary, occasional affair. To be vital, worship is ongoing and continuous. The need to worship is built into our very being itself. One of the ten commandments reminds us "To remember the Sabbath day to keep it holy." When one does not come apart for worship, there is something that dries up within us and deadness begins to consume our life. We read in the New Testament "that Jesus went to the synagogue as his custom was." He had a habit of going to church week after week. He didn't go there just because he enjoyed the preaching, or he enjoyed the people, or they were friendly to him, or they were nice to him when he was a boy. It was "his custom" to go. Out of his own deep need for reverence, he weekly offered worship to his Father. Within each of us, there is a "plant" called reverence which needs watering weekly. We come to church because there is a deep need to worship God.

A Place for Community

The second reason I go to church is because of the need for community. In an article, "What to Do with the Nones?", Bill Wilson, drawing on conversations with Ryan Burge, Professor at Eastern Illinois University, notes that the church's response to the Nones' criticism is to "build community."[21] This sense of community may not be found in the sanctuary in Sunday worship but may be experienced in small groups that meet at other times and places during the week other than Sunday. The church needs to

---

21 Bill Wilson, "What to do with the nones?" Baptist News Global, December 2, 2022.

reach out toward its community rather than expecting persons to come for the church's programs.

Community or Fellowship is experienced on many levels. There is *local fellowship*. Where there is real fellowship, there will be friendship. Fellowship and friendship cannot be equated. But there is really nothing much worse than a church that is unfriendly, where people never speak to each other. A man went to worship in a church once during the summertime. He saw the advertisement on their bulletin board which read, "It's cool inside." When he walked out of the church, he went over to the board and wrote underneath these words: "Brother, you said it!" He wasn't speaking just about the temperature inside either, but about the way the people responded to him. He found no sense of interest or concern for him.

William Willimon told about a man who had been visiting his church and he had contacted him in hope that he would join. After he missed a couple of Sundays, he called him to ask if he had made a decision. "In the beginning I really liked your church;" the man responded. "I liked the worship services, and I enjoyed visiting in the church school classes. But frankly - I don't mean this as a criticism - the better I got to know your people, the more I disliked them."

What an indictment of the church. What did he discover? In many churches these people are negative and constantly complaining. Nothing suits them. There is no joy in being around them. If we encourage people to come to the church's community, then we need to be welcoming and affirming, not negative and critical. Where Christ is present in his church, there should be a real fellowship that expresses love, graciousness, and encouragement. A positive message is received that "Friends are here!" There is a real sense of family where one finds care and support in times of need.

But real community reaches beyond the local level. When you and I are in the fellowship of Christ, we are aware that it is a spiritual fellowship. Christian fellowship is not just getting together for meals and having socials, but it is a spiritual community where

Christ himself is Lord. The presence of Christ sustains the church. This is what the writer of the Book of Hebrews is talking about. He described the fellowship which Jesus Christ himself founded as "the church of the firstborn" (Heb. 12: 22-25). Christ is Lord. The key ingredient in any church's fellowship is the confession by each believer that Christ is Lord.

But the church is also *a universal community*. We join hands with other Christians who down through the ages have committed their lives in faith to Christ. You and I are part not only of a local community but are linked to the universal church - the church, which was founded by Christ where Peter, Mary Magdalene. Paul, Phoebe, Augustine, Luther, Calvin, Wesley, Lottie Moon, Annie Armstrong, Albert Schweitzer, Martin Luther King, Jr., and countless numbers have pledged their allegiance to Jesus Christ. Thousands of people in Africa, Russia, China, Japan, Europe and around the world are bound together in this universal church. Yes, the church is local but also timeless, international, interracial, and universal. I want to be a part of that kind of church.

I love to have a fire on a cold winter night. But one thing I learned a long time ago about fires is that if one of the logs falls away from the others, it soon begins to cool and loses it glow and warmth. That log has to be brought back in close to the others if it is to continue burning and generate heat. If one is separated from the warmth of the Christian fellowship, that life grows cool and lifeless. The fellowship sustains us.

The writer to Hebrews writes about "the sprinkling of blood" (Heb. 12:23) which reminds us that the church was founded on the death of Jesus Christ. He laid down his life for his church. It is a redeemed community. The church is never *my* church nor *your* church. It is Christ's church. It was Christ who died for his church. The church is a redeemed fellowship - a community committed to Christ. Where two or three are gathered together, he is in their midst. I come to the church, so I can be in that kind of fellowship.

The Church Provides an Opportunity to Experience God's Grace

My third reason for going to church is because the church is the medium that dispenses and shares the grace of God. Where else can you go to understand and find out about the grace of God other than the church? The church is the institution that carries the message of God forward. It is the institution that shares the good news of God with others. In church we are made aware of our own sinfulness, God's love, and salvation.

I am proud of the church, proud of its tradition. Down through the centuries it has been the agency - the medium - which has established schools, hospitals, children's homes, and great universities like Princeton and Harvard. They came out of the church's mission. I am proud of that kind of tradition. I know what the church has done for good through the centuries. I know of no one who wants to live in a community where there are no churches. Church always makes a difference for good in a community. I am proud of the church and its rich tradition.

Through the church community I first discovered God. As a child my parents brought me to church, and it was there I learned of God's grace and his redeeming power. It was there I first learned about the mission and ministry of the church. I am proud to perpetuate God's love through his institutional church. God's grace offers people a second chance, an opportunity to begin again.

I remember a man in my first congregation who looked like one of the roughest persons I had ever seen in my life. I was told that Johnny wasn't a Christian. I was asked as a very young minister if I would go by and talk with him. To be honest with you I felt very uncomfortable around Johnny. He was a great big old gruff-looking guy, and I wasn't sure what he might say or do. But I went by and talked to Johnny one day. I spoke to him about his need to give his life to Christ. Surprisingly to this young preacher he did. He committed his life to Christ, made a confession of faith in church, was baptized, and continued to come regularly to church. Years later, when I went back to preach in that little country church, Johnny was sitting in the pews with his family. He had made a commitment of his life to Christ, and he learned about that grace in church.

I received a telephone call from a young woman several years ago in one of my churches. She said she wanted to come and talk to me about the church. She had been listening to our services on the radio. She came by and indicated that she was not a Christian but wanted to become one. We talked about the saving grace of Christ, and she gave her heart to him. The next Sunday she made her confession of faith and united with our church community and has continued to be a faithful part of that community. A young teenager invited a friend who had not gone to church much in his life. He came to our church and learned about Christ, made a confession of faith, and continued to be a vital part of our youth group. These persons discovered Christ through his church where God's grace is dispensed. I come to church to be a part of the continuing work of Christ in the world.

A Vision for Life's Meaning

My fourth reason for coming to church is because it is here that a vision is lifted before us of what life can be like. I do not have to be crushed by sin, burdened by mediocrity, or live on the lowest plains. God calls us to the highest and best we can be. He calls us to climb our spiritual Mount Zion. He calls us to the top of Calvary and to measure our lives by the stature of Christ, to look at the possibilities of what we can be like as we commit our lives to Christ. He lifts our horizons to the highest and best. We can never be content to be our own judges, measure our own worth and values, but strive to reach for the standards which Christ lifts before us. As Isaiah had a vision of the Lord high and lifted up, we look upward to God for his vision of what we can be as we are challenged to reach higher. We are continuously being remade by forces that influence our lives. I come to church, so I might be enriched by the presence of Christ, his teachings, the church's rich tradition, and the constant challenge held before me to reach higher to be like our Lord.

Receive Strength for Life's Journey

Then finally I come to church because it is the place that gives me strength to face life's difficulties and tragedies. The church offers us hope in our brokenness. It offers us direction for our meaninglessness. It offers us support in our times of grief, depression, loneliness, and stress. It offers us friends who gather around to support us in times of divorce, and friends who encourage us and sustain us in times of sickness, pain, and grief. It offers us a community of fellowship that sustains us. It provides us a family that encircles us with its love and support.

When our nation went through the tragic loss of six astronauts and a young schoolteacher in the explosion of our space shuttle several years ago, our people came together in mourning. I didn't hear people saying: "Let me go off and be by myself." There was a call for togetherness. A time of national grief was proclaimed. We were asked to turn on our automobile headlights to indicate our common sorrow in this tragedy. We drew strength from each other. The church brings us together in a community, so we can find strength from each other and the presence of God to face the tragedies, burdens and hurts of life which we have insufficient strength to bear by ourselves. I have always found it sad to hold a funeral service for a family that has no church tradition, no church support group, because they have drifted away from the church or have never been a member of a church. In the time of greatest need, they have cut themselves off from their strongest support group - the church.

Leo Tolstoy came to a very difficult time in his life, and even contemplated suicide. He used to hide rope because he was afraid he might hang himself. But he found hope in the words that he had learned at church: "The eternal God is my refuge." Even in his darkest of days those words gave him strength to go on. Bit by bit he found his way back. These words of hope guided him back to inner peace and composure. I come to church because it is the place in society which offers me strength, encouragement, and support. No other institution can ever really do that.

As you are reading this, if you are not attending church now, or even if you are attending on a regular basis, I want to challenge you to join the church again. Join it again in your commitment to be more faithful in your worship. Join it again in seeking to be open to the leadership of God. Join it again in being more responsive to the high vision which God is calling you to be like. Recommit yourself to be a part of the authentic community of Christ which seeks to support and undergird one another. Be willing to lean upon the church in your times of need. Covenant together now in a silent commitment that you will walk more closely with Christ and work more faithfully through his church. I hope this day that you will make a silent prayer to love your church more and to serve God better through it. Remember Christ died for his Church. We ought to be willing to live for it.

What's Our Business Outside The Building?

The Church's Mission

Matthew 28:19-20; 2 Corinthians 5:18-20

Several years ago, I heard a parable which I have not forgotten. On one of the coasts of our country some lifeguards were charged with the responsibility of protecting the lives of the swimmers along that section of the beach. The lifeguards would launch their boats and row out when the waves were high and treacherous to save people when they were drowning. These lifeguards were very efficient. No waves were ever too high, no difficulty too great for them. One day they rescued a man from drowning, and this man was so grateful that he wanted to do something for the lifeguards. He decided to build a beautiful lifeguard station on the shore. It was a first-class building. It was air-conditioned and had all the comforts they could possibly want. It had a kitchen, den area with a television and comfortable beds. Soon the lifeguards spent more and more of their time in the beautiful house on the beach. People could be screaming for help in the water, but the lifeguards did not hear their cries because they were inside enjoying all the comforts of the lifeguard station.

To me this is a parable about the church. You think about it for a moment. The church was established to reach out and bring the message of salvation to those who do not know Jesus Christ as Lord. Often, we build beautiful buildings, as we have done. Religious people gather inside their beautiful buildings and enjoy the comfort and convenience but forget that they have been commissioned to go outside these buildings and reach persons who do not know Christ.

Our Scripture text from Matthew's Gospel today points this out very vividly. The disciples of Jesus had gathered on some unknown mountain to meet him after the resurrection. We do not know which mountain, but it was someplace in Galilee. Matthew does not mention the resurrection appearances of Jesus in Jerusalem. Suddenly Jesus appeared to the disciples. Paul writes that Jesus appeared to over five hundred people who had gathered there (1 Cor. 15:6). In that appearance, Jesus gave his disciples what you and I usually call the Great Commission. He charged his followers with their missionary responsibility. Look with me for a few moments at the message Jesus gave them.

CLAIM OF GREAT AUTHORITY

First, Jesus made a claim of great authority. He says, "All authority on heaven and earth has been given to me." What a tremendous claim! And this claim is echoed through the New Testament. You find this theme in many of Paul's epistles. I mention only two examples. Paul writes that the glorified Christ when raised from the dead was seated at the right hand of the Father and "is far above all rule and authority and power and dominion, and above every name that is named, not only in this age but also in that which is to come; and he has put all things under his feet" (Eph. 1:20-21). In another place Paul writes: "Therefore God has highly exalted him and bestowed on him the name, which is above every name, that at the name of Jesus every knee should bow, in heaven and on earth and under the earth, and every tongue confess that Jesus Christ is Lord, to the glory of God the Father" (Phil.

2:7-11). We can find other references in I Peter 1:21 and also in Hebrews 2:9. In the Book of Revelation, John states: "Worthy is the Lamb who was slain, to receive power and wisdom and might and honor and glory and blessing" (Rev. 5:12).

There is no question that the New Testament ascribes to Jesus Christ all authority. The interesting thing is that down through the ages since the coming of Jesus, persons have found that Jesus does make a tremendous claim on their lives. Kings, presidents, emperors, peasants, wealthy and poor persons, scholars and illiterates, poets, musicians, artists, scientists have all felt the tremendous claim of Jesus Christ. Lives have been transformed by this allegiance. "All authority," Jesus claims, "is mine." We, as Christians, gather in a place to worship and also acknowledge that we stand under his authority. He is Lord of our lives. We, too, acknowledge Christ's claim of authority on our lives.

An Announcement of Jesus' Commission

Secondly, we notice in this passage that Jesus gave the church an announcement of his commission. It is a shame that we do not have a verb in English for "disciple," because the key emphasis in verse nineteen is "make disciples." "As you are going," "as you are baptizing," "as you are teaching," are all subordinate to "make disciples." All of these verbs are participles. The imperative in Greek is "make disciples." We are charged to "make disciples."

We Assume Most Are Already Christians

How do the followers of Jesus make disciples? Jesus begins by saying, "As you are going." Jesus is assuming that anyone who is his disciple is going to share the good news of salvation with others. Why don't we go? Well, I think, for one thing, we assume that most everybody around us is already Christian. In surveys that have been taken in our country, almost everybody acknowledges that this is a Christian country. They have a naive assumption that in some way most people are already Christians. Many believe that being born in America in some hocus-pocus fashion makes them a Christian. George Gallop, Jr., several years ago did a survey in which a majority of Americans consider themselves to be Christians. He summarized his conclusion this way.

We boast Christianity as our faith, but many of us have not bothered to learn the basic biblical facts of this religion. Many of us dutifully attend church, but this act appears to have made us no less likely than an unchurched brethren to engage in unethical behavior.

We say we are Christians, but sometimes we do not show much love toward those who do not share our particular religious perspective. We say we rejoice in the good news that Jesus brought, but we are often strangely reluctant to share the gospel with others. In a typical day the average person stays in front of the T.V. set nearly 25 times longer than in prayer. We say we are believers, but perhaps we are only assenters.[22]

Maybe that is the reason evangelists like Billy Graham and others have said that the greatest mission field today may be inside the church and not outside. Some of those on the church rolls have been inoculated with a mild dose of Christianity and this has made them immune to the real thing. We often don't share the message with others because we assume that everybody is Christian and does not need the gospel.

You likely have heard the story about the preacher and one of his laymen who went to visit some homes in the neighborhood of the church. As they pulled up in front of the house they were going to visit, they saw two Cadillacs and a Mercedes in the driveway, along with a big boat. They walked toward the door and saw the man sitting in front of his huge television set drinking a can of beer as he watched a ball game. The layman looked over at the preacher and asked, "What good news do we have to share with this man?"

---

22 George Gallup, Jr. and George O'Connell, What Do Americans Say that I AM (Philadelphia: Westminster, 1986), 88-89.

That is where we are in our modern society today, isn't it? If a person is wealthy, healthy, and wise, many feel we have no good news for them. We assume that these people are Christians. We know nothing about the brokenness, fragmentation, and lost condition in their lives. We assume these people are Christians, when they may be without purpose, meaning, forgiveness, hope, and love. Many long for wholeness and faith. We have a word they need to hear.

WE ARE TIMID

Sometimes we are really afraid to talk to others. We would like to but are really timid about taking that step. I know this feeling. As a young Minister, I would sometimes go visit somebody who was supposed to be a prospect for our church, who was not a Christian, and I knew I had to talk with them. I would knock on the door and sometimes I would pray silently to myself: "Oh, Lord, don't let them be at home." We all have those kinds of feelings of timidity at times.

EMBARRASSED BY SOME EVANGELISM METHODS

Sometimes we do not share the good news with others because we are embarrassed by some of the approaches which some evangelists have used. We are uncomfortable with some preacher standing in a person's face shaking a Bible, grabbing them by the lapel, or using some gosh-awful pious language and images that we don't like. We often refuse to do anything, because we don't want to be associated with these negative ways.

DON'T KNOW WHAT TO SAY

Sometimes we don't share the good news because we just don't know what to say. We really feel like we haven't been trained. Several years ago, I have done training programs in former churches where I have been pastor or interim pastor to help equip people to share the good news more effectively. All Christians need to be trained.

Why Share the Gospel?

The Command of Our Lord

Why should we share the good news of Jesus Christ with others? First, because it is the command of Christ. In our text we are commanded to make disciples. Jesus called his disciples to be fishers of men and women. Jesus, said, "You are to be my witnesses." In the passage that we read from Corinthians, we are reminded that we are to be "ambassadors for Christ." You and I are called to tell others about Christ. Evangelism/missions are the responsibility of every Christian, not just the pastor and staff. The church would have died out a long time ago if only the professional clergy were charged to witness to the faith. If you are a Christian, you share the responsibility of bearing the good news of Christ to other persons. Every Christian is an evangelist.

Oh, I love the story about the woman who came back into her house after talking to a man who had knocked on the door. After he left, her husband asked, "What did he want?" "Oh, he wanted to know if I were Christian," the wife said. "Why didn't you tell him it was none of his business?" the husband replied. "If you had heard him talk," the wife answered, "you would have thought it was his business." Evangelism/missions are your business and mine. It is the business of all Christians to share the good news of Christ with others.

Our Concern for Others

Why do we want to share the good news of Christ with other people? A second reason is our sense of concern for others who have not heard the saving knowledge of Christ. If you and I have experienced the forgiving grace of God, why would we not want

Sharing the Good News

to share this wonderful news with others, who also need to have that experience of forgiveness and grace? Would we not want to share this message out of a sense of the love and joy which we have experienced from Christ? Having experienced God's abundant love, surely, we will want to tell others about that love.

Suppose I had found a cure for cancer, and you were in the hospital dying with cancer and I came to see you. Suppose I came into your room and fluffed up your pillow and talked to you about the UNC, NC State, Wake Forest, UVA, or VA Tech football games. Suppose I continued to talk with you about the weather, our mutual friends, or other matters, but never shared my cure for cancer with you. What would you think? We are charged with a mission to bear the good news of Christ with others—"as you are going make disciples." Several years ago at a CBF national meeting in Memphis, Tennessee, we heard from numerous persons who are serving as CBF missionaries around the world and in our own country. These are persons who are committed to sharing the Good News "as they are going."

As You Are Baptizing

But also, Jesus said, "As you are baptizing, make disciples." We are baptizing persons who have committed their lives to Christ. Baptism is a dramatic parable about the radical change in a person's life. In the early church, we see numerous ways the disciples witnessed for Christ. One way was through preaching and teaching. They often started preaching in the synagogues and when they could no longer do that, they would preach on street corners, or any place people would listen. They also would bear personal witness to Christ. When Andrew met Jesus, he went immediately and told Simon Peter, his brother, about Jesus. When Philip met Jesus, he in turn told Nathaniel. The disciples were busy telling others about Jesus. They also went from one house to another sharing the news about Jesus Christ. Sometimes a church service was held in somebody's house (Acts 20:20; 10:27-28; 16:15). The disciples likewise shared out of their own personal experience their story about what Christ had done for them. That which they had seen and heard, they told about it. (I John 1:1-3). Paul continuously told his conversion story (Acts 22:1-21). Later the disciples would share through literary means—the gospels—their witness to Christ. Paul wrote many letters to bear witness to the faith. We all can witness in a variety of ways.

In What Way Did They Share the Faith?

How did they share their faith? They shared the gospel wherever they met people and with whatever opportunities they had. Paul and Peter spoke in the synagogues. They spoke about Christ in the home of Cornelius or at the gate of the temple. They witnessed to Christ in a jail, in the marketplace, on Mars Hill in Athens, on the roadside or in a home. They utilized any occasion they had.

How did they share the gospel? They did it with enthusiasm. They spoke with so much enthusiasm that one time they were accused of being drunk (Acts 2:13). You recall the story in Acts. The disciples were excited about what God had done in Jesus Christ and were filled with the Spirit. The disciples also were courageous in their witness. Stephen was stoned as he bore witness to Christ. Paul suffered much persecution to carry the message of Christ to others. The disciples also drew on the Scriptures as their source of authority. They frequently quoted from the Old Testament to show how it pointed to Jesus as the Messiah. They always pointed men and women to Jesus Christ and the difference he could make in their lives.

Alexander Whyte was a noted preacher at St. George's Church in Edinburgh. One day a man came by to see him. On Sunday he had invited a friend to come to church with him. Rigby, a commercial traveler, often visited Edinburgh on business. He would stay at a local hotel. He always invited some stranger to come with him to church. The man he invited on Sunday at first refused but later at Rigby's persistence came with him. The man was so overtaken by Whyte's preaching that he came back that night and silently made a commitment of faith to Jesus Christ. Rigby shared that news with Mr. Whyte.

"God bless you for telling me," Whyte said. "I thought Sunday night's sermon fell flat and I was very depressed about it." And then Whyte said: "I didn't quite catch your name." 'Rigby,' the man said. 'Rigby," responded Whyte, "I have been looking for you for years." He ran back into his study and came out with a huge stack of letters. He told him that he had letters from numerous men who told him about being invited to church by a man named Rigby. In his bundle of letters, twelve came from young men, four of whom had committed their lives to the ministry. All of this came about because one man invited others to church. Like this man, whatever opportunities you and I have, we need to use them to point others to Christ.

As You Teach

"Make disciples as you teach," Jesus said. One of the primary ministries of the church is to teach. Our purpose is to make disciples not just converts. Converts need to become disciples. Converts need to grow in their knowledge of the faith. We have too many people who are still right where they were when they became a Christian. They haven't grown. They are still baby Christians. We see this all the time in the church.

I have talked to a number of ministers over the years who say that one of the criticisms they often hear is: "We are leaving, because we are not being fed." What the ministers have discovered is that these people are upset because they are not being fed what they want to hear. They want religious pabulum. Many want sermons to focus on how to be converted. That theme, they think, doesn't touch them. They have already heard that. William H. Hinson, senior pastor of First United Methodist Church in Houston, Texas, observed: Oftentimes I have felt like saying to such persons, "Why don't you take the cross off the altar and replace it with a feeding trough? If your only concern is to fill your own spiritual bellies, and if you have no concern for the issues that tear our world apart, why not remove the cross from the altar?"[23]

What is Hinson saying? I think he means that there is a genuine concern to be fed that one might grow and deepen in his or her knowledge of the Christian faith. But some people want to continue to be breast-fed Christians. They want only the milk and not the meat of the word. Their focus in religion is often only as self-interest and what religion can do for them. They are upset at the hard sayings and demands of Jesus, and Paul's writings remain very difficult for them to comprehend. They want the candy, apples, and the sweetness of the faith, but they don't want to deal with the cross and its call for sacrifice and self-sacrificing commitment. Taking up the cross, however, is a radical part of what it means to follow Jesus Christ. It is tragic for someone to enter the doorway of conversion and stop at the entrance and refuse to continue growing.

I am thankful that when I made my commitment to Jesus Christ as Lord I had ministers, teachers, and friends who would not let me rest on my spiritual oars but challenged me to think and grow in the faith. They helped me to see what Jesus Christ has come to challenge me to be and become. We should never settle for clichés and slogans about our faith. Jesus Christ wants to pull us forward to wrestle with the toughest questions of life. Baptizing people is not the end but the beginning of a lifetime of learning about Christ and his way. One of the primary obligations of the pulpit and the church is to teach Christians how to grow in the faith. We are challenged to spend a life time learning about the life, death, resurrection and teachings of Jesus. Paul's teachings, the great doctrines of the faith and the meaning and witness of the Church are a part of the knowledge we seek to understand.

Evangelism Is Not Limited to Words

Evangelism is not limited to speaking about Christ. Sometimes the most effective way to reach someone for Christ is to

---
23 William H. Hinson, *A Place to Dig in* (Nashville: Abingdon Press, 1987).

meet a personal need in their life. It is hard to speak to someone about Christ when they are dying from hunger or have some other physical need. We may need first to give them food or meet some other need in their lives before we talk to them. A cup of cold water or some clothing may open a closed door. If we try only words and refused to put action to our words, then we may leave the beggar at the gate, the woman at the well, the blind in their darkness, the deaf in their soundless world, the lame in their paralysis, the hungry in their want, the poor in their poverty, the hopeless in their despondency, the inmates in their prison, or the hurting man or woman beside their road. Meeting human need and confronting genuine needs are an essential means of evangelism and missions. Both words and actions are needed for genuine evangelism. Words are seldom enough. James reminds us, "So with faith; if it does not lead to action, it is in itself a lifeless thing" (James 2: 17 New English Bible).

A Continuous Presence

Finally, Jesus gives us assurance of a continuous presence. First, Jesus assures us of a personal presence. "I am with you always." "I am." "I am" echoes throughout the Gospel of John. "I am the Bread of Life.' "I am Light of the world." "I am the true vine." "I am the resurrection." "I am with you always." But Jesus states that he is also an abiding presence. "I am with you always." Jesus Christ, through the power of the Holy Spirit, is always with us no matter what the circumstances of life might be. When we seek to bear witness to our faith, Jesus Christ, through God's Spirit, is there helping us make that witness. Jesus is also the triumphant presence. "I am with you until the end of the ages." History will not come to an end with a whimper without direction and guidance. However history ends, we know that God is in control of history.

Dear friends, we can be thankful that we can gather together in churches of such beauty, and be in places where we have an opportunity to learn by the dedicated teaching of our Sunday

School teachers and others. But we need to remember that our major mission, after we have worshiped together, is to go into the world and share the good news of Jesus Christ with other persons.

During the Second World War when Helmut Thielicke was pastor in Stuttgart, Germany, the allied forces were bombing the city severely. One night a group of men had descended into a cellar for protection from the falling bombs. The next morning when Pastor Thielicke arrived on the scene, there was a gaping hole where the cellar had been. A woman came over to the minister and asked, "Are you Pastor Thielicke?" When he said he was, she said, "My husband was down there last night (as she pointed to the hole). All they found of him was his cap. We heard you preach. I want to thank you for getting him ready for eternity."

We are all preparing for eternity. God give us the courage and the joy to share the good news of Christ which we have experienced so that all persons will know.

www.ingramcontent.com/pod-product-compliance
Lightning Source LLC
Chambersburg PA
CBHW030943090426
42737CB00007B/525